THE BOOK OF MASKS

THE BOOK OF MASKS

THE BOOK OF MASKS

BY

REMY DE GOURMONT

TRANSLATED BY

JACK LEWIS

INTRODUCTION BY

LUDWIG LEWISOHN

EDITED BY

WILLIAM MANN

mannwilliam.org

Designed and Edited by William Mann
© 2021 mannwilliam.org
ISBN 9798749193800

CONTENTS

INTRODUCTION

To take critical questions seriously, even passionately, is one of the marks of a genuinely civilized society. It points to both personal disinterestedness and to an imaginative absorption in fundamentals. The American who watches eagerly some tilt in that great critical battle which has gone on for ages and has now reached our shores, is released from his slavery to the immediate and the parochial; he has ceased to flinch at the free exercise of thought; he has begun to examine his mind as his fathers examined only their conscience; he is a little less concerned for speed and a little more for direction; he is almost a philosopher and has risen from mere heated gregariousness to voluntary co-operation in a spiritual order. His equipment is, as a rule, still meagre, and so his partisanship is not always an instructed one. He may be overwhelmed by the formidable philosophical apparatus of one critic or merely irritated by the political whims of another. Hence nothing could well be more helpful to him than an introduction to a foreign critic who is at once a stringent thinker and a charming writer, who permitted his insight to be obscured by neither moral nor political prejudices, who is both urbane and incisive, catholic and discriminating.

Remy de Gourmont, like all the very great critics—Goethe, Ste. Beuve, Hazlitt, Jules Lemaitre—knew the creative instinct and exercised the creative faculty. Hence he understood, what the mere academician, the mere scholar, can never grasp, that literature is life grown flame-like and articulate; that, therefore, like life itself, it varies in aim and character, in form and colour and savor and is the memorable record of and commentary upon each stage in that great process of change that we call the world. To write like the Greeks or the Elizabethans or the French classics is precisely what we must not do. It would be both presumptuous and futile. All that we have to contribute to mankind, what is it but just— our selves? If we were duplicates of our great-grandfathers we would be littering the narrow earth to no enriching purpose; all we have to contribute to literature is, again, our selves. This moment, this sensation, this pang, this thought—this little that is intimately our own is all we have of the unique and precious and incomparable. Let us express it beautifully, individually, memorably and it is all we can do; it is all that the classics did in their day. To imitate the classics—be one! That is to say, live widely, intensely, unsparingly and record your experience in some timeless form. This, in brief, is the critical theory of Gourmont, this is the background of that startling and yet, upon reflection, so clear and necessary saying of his "The only excuse a man has for writing is that he express himself, that he reveal to others the kind of world reflected in the mirror of his soul; his only excuse is that he be original".

Gourmont, like the Symbolists whom he describes in this volume, founded his theory of the arts upon a metaphysical speculation. He learned from the German idealists, primarily the Post-Kantians and Schopenhauer, that the world is only our representation, only our individual vision and that, since there is no criterion of the existence or the character of an external reality, that vision is, of course, all we actually have to express in art. But to accept his critical theory it is not necessary to accept his metaphysical views. The variety of human experience remains equally infinite and equally fascinating on account of its very infiniteness, whatever its objective content may or may not be. We can dismiss that antecedent and insoluble question and still agree that the best thing a man can give in art as in life is his own self. What kind of a self? One hears at once the hot and angry question of the conservative critic. A disciplined one, by all means, an infinitely and subtly cultivated one.

But not one shaped after some given pattern, not a replica, not a herd-animal, but a human personality. But achieving such personalities, the reply comes, people fall into error. Well, this is an imperfect universe and the world-spirit, as Goethe said, is more tolerant than people think.

It is clear that criticism conceived of in this fashion, can do little with the old methods of harsh valuing and stiff classification. If, as Jules, Lemaitre put it, a poem, a play, a novel, "exists" at all, if it has that fundamental veracity of experience and energy of expression which raise it to the level of literary discussion, a critic like Gourmont cannot and will not pass a classifying judgment on it at all. For such judgments involve the assumption that there exists a fixed scale of objective values. And for such a scale we search both the world and the mind in vain. Hence, too—and this is a point of the last importance—we are done with arbitrary exclusions, exclusions by transitory conventions or by tribal habits lifted to the plane of eternal laws. All experience, the whole soul of man—nothing less than that is now our province. And no one has done more to bring us that critical and creative freedom and enlargement of scope than Remy de Gourmont.

In the volume before us, for instance, he discusses writers of very varied moods and interests. Dr. Samuel Johnson or, for that matter, a modern preceptist critic, speaking of these very poets, would have told us how some of them were noble and some ignoble and certain ones moral and others no better than they should be. And both of these good and learned and arrogant men would have instructed Verlaine in what to conceal, and Gustave Kahn in how to build verses and Régnier in how to enlarge the range of his imagery. Thus they would have missed the special beauty and thrill that each of these poets has brought into the world. For they read—as all their kind reads—not with peace in their hearts but with a bludgeon in their hands. But if we watch Gourmont who had, by the way, an intellect of matchless energy, we find that he read his poets with that wise passiveness which Wordsworth wanted men to cultivate before the stars and hills. He is uniformly sensitive; he lets his poets play upon him; he is the lute upon which their spirits breathe. And then that lute itself begins to sound and to utter a music of its own which swells and interprets and clarifies the music of his poets and brings nearer to us the wisdom and the loveliness which they and he have brought into the world.

Thus it is, first of all, as one of the earliest and finest examples of the New Criticism that this English version of the "Book of Masks" is to be welcomed. For the New Criticism is the chief phenomenon in that movement toward spiritual and moral tolerance which the world so sorely needs. But the book is also to be welcomed and valued for the sake of its specific subject matter. One movement in the entire range of modern poetry and only one surpasses the movement of the French Symbolists in clearness of beauty, depth of feeling, wealth and variety of music. This Symbolist movement arose in France as a protest against the naturalistic, the objective in substance and against the rigid and sonorous in form. Eloquence had so long, even during the romantic period, dominated French poetry that profound inwardness of inspiration and lyrical fluidity of expression were regarded as essential by the literary reformers of the later eighteen hundred and eighties. It was in the service of these ends that Stéphane Mallarmé taught the Symbolist system Of poetics: to name no things except as symbols of unseen realities, to use the external world merely as a means of communicating mood and revery and reflection. The doctrine and the verse of Mallarmé spoke to a Europe that was under the sway of a similar reaction and the work of poets as diverse as Arthur Symons, William Butler Yeats and Hugo von Hofmannsthal is unthinkable without the pervasive influence of the French master. Mallarmé and his doctrine are, indeed, the starting point of all modern lyrical poetry. Whatever has been written since, in free verse or fixed, betrays through conformity or re-action, the mark of that doctrine and the resultant movement.

The actual poets of the movement are little known among us. Verlaine's name is already almost a classical one and the exquisite versions of many of his poems by Arthur Symons are accessible; Verhaeren was lifted into a brief notoriety some years ago. But who really reads the stormy and passionate verses of the Flemish master? Nor are there many who have entered the suave and golden glow that radiates from Régnier, chief of the living poets of France, or who have vibrated to the melancholy of Samain or the inner music of Francis Vielé-Griffin. The other poets, less copious and less applauded, are not greatly inferior in the quality of their best work. There is not a poet in Gourmont's book who has not written some verses that add permanently to the world's store of living beauty. Nor is it true that a slightly more recent development in French poetry has surpassed the works of the Symbolists. M. Francis Jammes writes with a charming simplicity and M. Paul Fort with a large rhythmic line, with freshness and with grace and the very young "unanimiste" poets are intellectual and tolerant and sane. But they are all, in the essentials of poetry, children of the Symbolists whose work remains the great modern contribution of France to poetical literature.

LUDWIG LEWISOHN.

It is difficult to characterize a literary evolution in the hour when the fruits are still uncertain and the very blossoming in the orchard unconsummated. Precocious *trees*, slow-developing and dubious trees which one would not care, however, to call sterile: the orchard is very diverse and rich, too rich. The thickness of the leaves brings shadow, and the shadow discolours the flowers and dulls the hues of the fruit.

We will stroll through this rich, dark orchard and sit down for a moment at the foot of the strongest, fairest, and most agreeable trees.

Literary evolutions receive a name when they merit it by importance, necessity and fitness. Quite often, this name has no precise meaning, but is useful in serving as a rallying sign to all who accept it, and as the aiming point for those who attack it. Thus the battle is fought around a purely verbal labarum. What is the meaning of *Romanticism?* It is easier to feel than to explain it. What is the meaning of *Symbolism?* Practically nothing, if we adhere to the narrow etymological sense. If we pass beyond, it may mean individualism in literature, liberty in art, abandonment of taught formulas, tendencies towards the new and strange, or even towards the bizarre. It may also mean idealism, a contempt for the social anecdote, anti-naturalism, a propensity to seize only the characteristic details of life, to emphasize only those acts that distinguish one man from another, to strive to achieve essentials; finally, for the poets symbolism seems allied to free verse, that is, to unswathed verse whose young body may frolic at ease, liberated from embarrassments of swaddling clothes and straps.

But all this has little affinity with the syllables of the word, for we must not let it be insinuated that symbolism is only the transformation of the old allegory or of the art of personifying an idea in a human being, a landscape, or a narrative. Such an art is the whole of art, art primordial and eternal, and a literature freed from this necessity would be unmentionable. It would be null, with as much aesthetic significance as the clucking of the hocco or the braying of the wild ass.

Literature, indeed, is nothing more than the artistic development of the idea, the imaginary heroes. Heroes, or men (for every man in his sphere is a hero), are only sketched by life; it is art which perfects them by giving them, in exchange for their poor sick souls, the treasure of an immortal idea, and the humblest, if chosen by a great poet, may be called to this participation. Who so humble as that Aeneas whom Virgil burdens with all the weight of being the idea of Roman force, and who so humble as that Don Quixote on whom Cervantes imposes the tremendous load of being at once Roland, the four sons Aymon, Amadis, Palmerin, Tristan and all the knights of the Round Table! The history of symbolism would be the history of man himself, since man can only assimilate a symbolized idea. Needless to insist on this, for one might think that the young devotees of symbolism are unaware of the *Vita Nuova* and the character Beatrice, whose frail, pure shoulders nevertheless keep erect under the complex weight of symbols with which the poet overwhelms her.

Whence, then, came the illusion that symbolizing of the idea was a novelty?

In these last years, we had a very serious attempt of literature based on a scorn of the idea, a disdain of the symbol. We are acquainted with its theory, which seems culinary: take a slice of life, etc. Zola, having invented the recipe, forgot to serve it. His "slices of life" are heavy poems of a miry, tumultuous lyricism, popular romanticism, democratic symbolism, but ever full of an idea, always pregnant with allegoric meaning. The idealistic revolt, then, did not rear itself against the works (unless against the despicable works) of naturalism, but against its theory, or rather against its pretension; returning to the eternal, antecedent necessities of art, the rebels presumed to express new and even surprising truths in professing their wish to reinstate the idea in literature; they only relighted the torch; they also lighted, all around, many small candles.

There is, nevertheless, a new truth, which has recently entered literature and art, a truth quite metaphysical and quite *a priori* (in appearance), quite young, since it is only a century old, and truly new, since it has not yet served in the aesthetic order. This evangelical and marvelous truth, liberating and renovating, is the principle the world's ideality. With reference to th thinking subject, man, the world, everything that is external, only exists according to the idea he forms of it. We only know phenomena, we only reason from appearances; all truth in itself escapes us; the essence is unassailable. It is what Schopenhauer has popularized under this so simple and clear formula: the world is my representation. I do not see that which is; that which is, is what I see. As many thinking men, so many diverse and perhaps dissimilar worlds. This doctrine, which Kant left on the way to be flung to the rescue of the castaway morality, is so fine and supple that one transposes it from theory to practice without clashing with logic, even the most exigent. It is a universal principle of emancipation for every man capable of understanding. It has only revolutionized aesthetics, but here it is a question only of aesthetics.

Definitions of the beautiful are still given in manuals; they go farther; formulas are given by which artists attain the expression of the beautiful. There are institutes for teaching these formulas, which are but the average and epitome of ideas or of preceding appreciations. Theories in aesthetics generally being obscure, the ideal paragon, the model, is joined to them. In those institutes (and the civilized world is but a vast Institute) all novelty is held blasphemous, all personal affirmation becomes an act of madness. Nordau, who has read, with bizarre patience, all contemporary literature, propagated this idea, basely destructive of all individualism, that "nonconformity" is the capital crime of a writer. We violently differ in opinion. A writer's capital crime is conformity, imitativeness, submission to rules and precepts. A writer's work should be not only the reflection, but the magnified reflection of his personality. The only excuse a man has for writing, is to express himself, to reveal to others the world reflected in his individual mirror; his only excuse is to be original. He should say things not yet said, and say them in a form not yet formulated. He should create his own aesthetics, and we should admit as many aesthetics as there are original minds, judging them according to what they are not.

Let us then admit that symbolism, though excessive, unseasonable and pretentious, is the expression of individualism in art.

This too simple but clear definition will suffice provisionally. In the course of the following portraits, or later, we doubtless will have occasion to complete it. Its principle will, nevertheless, serve to guide us, by inciting us to investigate, not what the new writers should have done, according to monstrous rules and tyrannical traditions, but what they wished to do. Aesthetics has also become a personal talent; no one has the right to impose it upon others. An artist can be compared with himself alone, but there is profit and justice in noting dissimilarities. We will try to mark, not how the "newcomers" resemble each other, but how they differ, that is to say in what way they exist, for to exist is to be different.

This is not written to pretend that among most of them are no evident similarities of thought and technique, an inevitable fact, but so inevitable that it is without interest. No more do we insinuate that this flowering is spontaneous; before the flower comes the seed, itself fallen from a flower. These young people have fathers and masters: Baudelaire, Villiers de l'Isle-Adam, Verlaine, Mallarmé, and others. They love them dead or alive, they read them, they listen to them. What stupidity to think that we disdain those of yesterday! Who then has a more admired and affectionate court than Stéphane Mallarmé? And is Villiers forgotten? And Verlaine forsaken?

Now, we must warn that the order of these portraits, without being altogether arbitrary, implies no classification of prize-lists. There are, even, outside of the gallery, absent personages, whom we will bring back on occasion. There are empty frames and also bare places. As for the portraits themselves, if any one judges them incomplete and too brief, we reply that we wished them so, having the intention only to give indications, only to show, with the gesture of an arm, the way.

Lastly, to join today with yesterday, we have intercalated familiar faces among the new figures: and then, instead of rewriting a physiognomy known to many, we have tried to bring to light some obscure point, rather than the whole.

THE BOOK OF MASKS

MAURICE MAETERLINCK

Of the life lived by sad beings who stir in the mystery of a night. They know nothing save to smile, to suffer, to love; when they wish to understand, the effort of their disquietude grows to anguish, their revolt vanishes in sobbings. To mount, forever to mount the mournful steps of Calvary and beat the brow against an iron door: so mounts Sister Ygraine, so mounts and beats against the cruel iron gate each of the poor creatures whose simple and pure tragedies Maeterlinck reveals to us.

In other times the meaning of life was known; then men were not ignorant of the essential; since they knew the end of their journey, and in what last inn they would find the bed of repose. When, by science itself, this elementary science had been taken from them, some rejoiced, believing themselves delivered of a burden; others grieved, feeling clearly that above all the other burdens on their shoulders, one had been thrown, itself heavier than all the rest: the burden of Doubt.

A whole literature has been begotten of this sensation, a literature of grief, revolt against the burden, blasphemies against the mute God. But, after the fury of their cries and interrogations, there was a remission, and this was the literature of sadness, uneasiness and anguish; revolt has been declared useless and imprecation puerile. Made wise by vain struggles, humanity slowly resigns itself to knowing nothing, comprehending nothing, fearing nothing, hoping for nothing—except the very remote.

There is an island somewhere in the mists, and in the island is a château, and in the château is a great room lit by a little lamp, and in the great room people are waiting. What do they await? They know not. They are expecting someone to knock at the door, they expect the lamp to go out, they expect Death. They converse; yes, they speak words which for an instant trouble the silence. Then they listen again, leaving their phrases unended and their gestures interrupted. They listen, they wait. She will perhaps not come? Oh! she will come. She always comes. It is late, she will perhaps not come till the morrow. And the people gathered in the great room beneath the little lamp begin to laugh and go on hoping. Someone knocks. And that is all; it is a whole life; it is the whole of life.

In this sense, Maeterlinck's dramas, so deliciously unreal, are deeply alive and true; his characters, with the appearance of phantoms, are steeped with life, like those seemingly inert balls, which, when charged with electricity, grow fulgent at the contact of a point; they are not abstractions but syntheses; they are states of soul or, better still, states of humanity, moments, minutes which shall be eternal. In short, they are real, by dint of their unreality.

A like kind of art was formerly practiced, after the *Roman de la Rose*, by the pious romancers who, in little books of pretentious clumsiness, made symbols and abstractions revolve. Bunyan's *Pilgrim's Progress, Le Voyage Spirituel*, by the Spaniard Palafox, *le Palais de l'Amour divin*, by an unknown person, are not altogether contemptible works, but things there are truly too explicit and the characters bear names that are truly too evident. Does one, in any free theater, see a drama played by beings called Courage, Hate, Joy, Silence, Care, Longing, Fear, Anger, and Shame? The hour of such amusement has passed or has not returned: do not re-read *le Palais de l'Amour divin*; read *la Mort de Tintagiles*, for it is of the new work that we must ask for these aesthetic pleasures, if we desire them complete, poignant and enveloping. Maeterlinck, truly, takes, pierces and entwines us in Octupi formed of the delicate hair of young sleeping princesses, and in the midst of them the troubled sleep of the little child, "sad as a young king". He entwines and bears us where he pleases, to the very depths of the abyss where whirls "the decomposed corpse of Alladin's lamb", and farther, to the pure dark regions where lovers say:

> Kiss me gravely. Close not the eyes when I kiss you so. I want
> to see the kisses that tremble in your heart; and the dew that
> mounts from your soul . . . We shall not find more kisses like
> these . . .—Evermore, evermore! . . .—No, no: one does not kiss
> twice on the heart of death.

Before such delicate sighings, all objection grows mute; one is silent at having felt a new way of loving and expressing love. New, truly. Maeterlinck is very much himself, and to remain entirely personal he can be a monochord; but he has sown, steeped and scutched the hemp for this one cord, and it sings gently, sadly, uniquely under his drooping hands. He has achieved a true work; he has found an unheard muffled cry, a kind of lamentation, coldly mystical.

The word mysticism during these last years has taken such diverse and even divergent meanings that it must be clearly and newly defined each time one writes it. Certain persons give it a significance which would draw it to that other word which seems clear, individualism. It is certain that it touches the other, since mysticism may be called the state in which a soul, abandoning the physical world and scornful of its shocks and accidents, gives its mind only to relations and direct intimacies with the infinite. But, if the infinite is changeless and one, souls are changing and many. A soul has not the same communications with God as has his sister, and God, though changeless and one, is modified by the desire of each of his creatures and does not tell one what he has told another. Liberty is the privilege of the soul raised to mysticism. The body itself is but a neighbor to whom the soul scarcely gives the friendly counsel of silence, but if the body speaks, she hears it only as through a wall, and if the body acts, she sees it act through a mask. Another name has been historically given to such a state of life: quietism. This sentence of Maeterlinck is altogether that of a quietist who shows us God smiling "at our most serious faults as one smiles at the play of little dogs on a rug". This is serious but true if we think how tiny a thing a fact is, how a fact is caused, how we all are led by the endless chain of action, and how little we really participate in our most decisive and best considered acts. Such an ethics, leaving the care of useless judgments to wretched human laws, snatches from life its very essence and transports it to the upper regions where it blossoms, sheltered from contingencies and from the humiliations which social contingencies are. Mystic morality ignores everything not marked at the same time with the double seal of the human and divine. Wherefore, it was always feared by clergy and magistrates, for in denying every hierarchy of appearance, it denies, to the point of abstention, all social order. A mystic can consent to all bondages, except that of being a citizen. Maeterlinck sees the time drawing near when men will understand each other, soul to soul, in the same way that the mystic's soul communes with God. Is it true? Will men one day be men, proud, free beings who admit no other judgments than God's judgments? Maeterlinck perceives this dawn, because he gazes within himself and is himself a dawn, but if he watched external humanity, he would only see the impure, socialistic appetite of troughs and stables. The humble, for whom he has divinely written, will not read his book, and if they did read it they would see in it but a mockery, for they have learned that the ideal is a manger, and they know that their masters would flog them if they lifted their eyes to God.

So *le Trésor des Humbles*, that book of liberation and love, makes me think bitterly of the unhappy condition of man today—and doubtless in all possible times,

Magnifique mais qui sans espoir se délivre
Pour n'avoir pas chanté la region où vivre
Quand du stérile hiver a resplendi l'ennui.

Magnificent, but who without hopes delivers himself
for not having praised the country in which to live
when from the sterile winter ennui has grown resplendent.

And it will be in vain that

Tout son col secouera cette blanche agonie.

His neck will shake off this white agony.

the hour of deliverance will be past and only a few will have heard it sound.

Nevertheless, what means of hope in these pages where Maeterlinck, disciple of Ruysbroeck, Novalis, Emerson and Hello, only asking of these superior spirits (whose two lesser had intuitions of genius) the sign of the hand that stimulates mysterious voyages! The generality of men, and the more conscious, who have so many hours of indifference, would find here encouragement to enjoy the simplicity of days and muffled murmurs of deep life. They would learn the meaning of very humble gestures and very futile words, and that an infant's laugh or a woman's prattle equals, by what it holds of soul and mystery, the most resplendent words of sages. For Maeterlinck, with his air of being a sage, and quite wise, confidently narrates unusual thoughts with a frankness quite disrespectful of psychological tradition, and with a boldness quite contemptuous of mental habits, assumes the courage only to attribute to things the importance they will have in an ultimate world. Thus, sensuality is altogether absent in his meditations. He knows the importance, but also the insignificance of the stir of blood and nerves, storms that precede or follow, but never accompany thought. And if he speaks of women who are nothing but soul, it is to inquire into "the mysterious salt which forever conserves the memory of the touch of two lips".

Maeterlinck's literature, poems or philosophy, comes in an hour when we have most need to be fortified and strengthened, in an hour when it is not immaterial to learn that the supreme end of life is "to keep open the highways that lead from the visible to the invisible." Maeterlinck has not only kept open the highways frequented by so many good-intentioned souls, and where great-minded men here and there open their arms like oases. It rather seems that he has increased to infinity the extent of these highways; he has said "such specious words in low tones" that the brambles have made way of themselves, the trees have pruned themselves spontaneously, a step beyond is possible, and the gaze today travels farther than it did yesterday.

Others doubtless have or have had a richer language, a more fertile imagination, a clearer gift of observation, more fancy, faculties better fitted to trumpet the music of words. Granted; but with a timid and poor language, childish dramatic combinations, an almost enervating system of repetition in phraseology, with these awkwardnesses, with all his awkwardnesses, Maurice Maeterlinck works at books and booklets that have a certain originality, a novelty so truly new that it will long disconcert the lamentable troop of people who pardon audacity if there be a precedent—as in the protocol—but who hold in scorn genius, which is the perpetual audacity.

ÉMILE VERHAEREN

Of all the poets of today, narcissi along the river, Verhaeren is the least obliging in allowing himself to be admired. He is rude, violent, unskillful. Busied for twenty years in forging a strange and magical tool, he remains in a mountain cavern, hammering the reddened irons, radiant in the fire's reflection, haloed with sparks. Thus it is we should picture him, a forger who,

> Comme s'il travaillait l'acier des âmes,
> Martèle à grands coups pleins, les lames
> Immenses de la patience et du silence.

> As if he were fashioning the steel of souls,
> hammers with great full strokes, the immense plates
> of patience and silence.

If we discover his dwelling and question him, he replies with a parable whose every word seems scanned on the forge, and, to conclude, he delivers a tremendous blow of his heavy hammer.

When he is not laboring at his forge, he goes forth through the fields, head and arms bare, and the Flemish fields tell him secrets they have not yet told anyone. He beholds miraculous things and is not astonished at them. Singular beings pass before him, beings whom everybody jostles without being aware, visible alone to him. He has met the November Wind:

> Le vent sauvage de novembre.
> Le vent,
> L'avez-vous rencontré, le vent
> Au carrefour des trois cents routes . . . ?

> The savage wind of November,
> the wind,
> have you met it, the wind
> at the crossroads of three hundred paths . . . ?

He has seen Death, and more than once; he has seen Fear; he has seen Silence

> S'asseoir immensément du côté de la nuit.

> Seated gigantically on the side of the night.

The characteristic word of Verhaeren's poetry is *halluciné*. The word leaps from page to page. An entire collection, the *Campagnes hallucinées* has not freed him from this obsession. Exorcism was not possible, for it is the nature and very essence of Verhaeren to be the hallucinated poet. "Sensations," Taine said, "are true hallucinations." But where does truth begin or end? Who shall dare circumscribe it? The poet, with no psychological scruples, wastes no time over troubling himself to divide hallucinations into truths or untruths. For him they are all true if they are sharp and strong, and he recounts them frankly— and when the recitation is made by Verhaeren, it is very lovely. Beauty in art is a relative result which is achieved by the mixture of very different elements, often the most unexpected. Of these elements, one alone is stable and permanent, and ought to be found in all combinations: that is novelty. A work of art must be new, and we recognize it as such quite simply by the fact that it gives a sensation not yet experienced.

If it does not give this, a work, perfect though it be adjudged, is everything that is contemptible. It is useless and ugly, since nothing is more absolutely useful than beauty. With Verhaeren, beauty is made of novelty and strength. This poet is a strong man and, since those *Villes tentaculaires* which surged with the violence of a telluric upheaval, no one dares to deny him the state and glory of a great poet. Perhaps he has not yet quite finished the magic instrument which for twenty years he has been forging. Perhaps he is not yet master of his language. He is unequal; he lets his most beautiful pages grow heavy with inopportune epithets, and his finest poems become entangled in what was once called prosaism. Nevertheless, the impression of power and grandeur remains, and yes: he is a great poet. Listen to this fragment from *Cathédrales*:

> —O ces foules, ces foules
> Et la misère et la détresse qui les foulent
> Comme des houles!

> > —O these crowds, these crowds,
> > and the misery and distress that whips them
> > like billows.

> Les ostensoirs, ornés de soie,
> Vers les villes échafaudées,
> En toits de verre et de cristal,
> Du haut du choeur sacerdotal,
> Tendent la croix des gothiques idées.

> > Monstrances, decorated with silk,
> > towards the heaped up towns,
> > in roofs of glass and crystal,
> > from the height of the sacerdotal choir,
> > stretch the cross of gothic ideas.

> Ils s'imposent dans l'or des clairs dimanches
> —Toussaint, Noël, Pâques et Pentecôtes blanches.
> Ils s'imposent dans l'or et dans l'encens et dans la fête
> Du grand orgue battant du vol de ses tempêtes

> > They obtrude themselves in the gold of clear Sundays
> > —All Saints' day, Christmas, Easter, and white Pentecosts.
> > They obtrude themselves in the gold and incense and the fête
> > of the great organ beating with the flight of its storms.

Les chapiteaux rouges et les voûtes vermeilles,
Ils sont une âme, en du soldi,
Qui vit de vieux décor et d'antique mystère
Autoritaire.

    The red capitals and vermillion vaults
    are a soul, in sunlight,
    living in the old background and antique mystery
    authoritarian.

Pourtant, dès que s'éteignent le cantique
Et l'antienne naïve et prismatique,
Un deuil d'encens évaporé s'empreint
Sur les trépieds d'argent et les autels d'airain,

    Yet, when the song
    a grief of incense evaporated stamps itself
    on the golden tripods and brazen altars.
    and the naive, prismatic anthem ceases,

Et les vitraux, grands de siècles agenouillés
Devant le Christ, avec leurs papes immobiles
Et leurs martyrs et leurs héros, semblent trembler
Au bruit d'un train hautain que passe sur la ville.

    And the stained glass windows, lofty with ages
    kneeling before Christ, with their immobile popes
    and martyrs and heroes, seem to tremble
    at the sound of a proud train passing through the town.

Verhaeren appears a direct son of Victor Hugo, especially in his earliest works. Even after his evolution towards a poetry more freely feverish, he still remains romantic. Here, to explain this, are four verses evoking the days of former times.

Jadis—c'était la vie errante et somnambule,
A travers les matins et les soirs fabuleux,
Quand la droite de Dieu vers les Chanaans bleus
Traçait la route d'or au fond des crépuscules.

    Formerly—there was the errant, somnambulous life,
    across the mornings and fabulous evening,
    when the right hand of God towards the blue Canaans
    traced the golden road in the depth of the shadows.

Jadis—c'était la vie énorme, exaspérée,
Sauvagement pendue aux crins des étalons,
Soudaine, avec de grands éclairs à ses talons
Et vers l'espace immense immensément cabrée.

      Formerly—there was the enormous, exasperated life,
      fiercely hung on the manes of stallions,
      suddenly, with great sparks from their hoofs,
      and towards immense space immensely provoked.

Jadis—c'était la vie ardent, évocatoire;
La Croix blanche de ciel, la Croix rouge d'enfer
Marchaient, à la clarté des armures de fer,
Chacune à travers sang, vers son ciel de victoire.

      Formerly—there was the ardent, evocative life;
      the white Cross of heaven, the red Cross of hell
      advanced, to the splendour of iron armors,
      each across blood, towards his victorious heaven.

Jadis—c'était la vie écumante et livide,
Vécue et morte, à coups de crime et de tocsins,
Bataille entre eux, de proscripteurs et d'assassins,
Avec, au-dessus d'eux, la mort folle et splendid.

      Formerly—there was the foaming livid life,
      alive and dead, with strokes of crime and tocsins,
      battle between them, of proscribers and assassins,
      with splendid and mad death above them.

These verses are drawn from *Villages illusoires*, written almost exclusively in assonant free verse, divided by means of a gasping rhythm, but Verhaeren, master of free verse, is also master of romantic verse, to which he can force, without being dashed to pieces, the unbridled, terrible gallop of his thought, drunk with images, phantoms and future visions.

HENRI DE RÉGNIER

He lives in an old Italian palace where emblems and figures are written on walls. He muses, passing from room to room. Towards evening he descends the marble stairs and goes into gardens flagged like streams, to dream of his life among fountain basins and ponds, while the black swans grow alarmed in their nests, and a peacock, alone like a king, seems to drink superbly the dying pride of a golden twilight. De Régnier is a melancholy, sumptuous poet. The two words which most often break forth in his verses are *or* and *mort* (gold and death) and there are poems where the insistence of this royal and autumnal rhyme returns and even induces fear. In the collection of his last works we could doubtless count more than fifty verses ending thus: golden birds, golden swans, golden basins, golden flowers, and dead lake, dead day, dead dream, dead autumn. It is a very curious obsession and symptomatic, not of a possible verbal poverty, rather the contrary, but of a confessed liking for a particularly rich colour and of a sad richness like that of a setting sun, a richness turning into the darkness of night.

Words obtrude themselves upon him when he wants to paint his impressions and the colour of his dreams; words also obtrude themselves upon whoever would define him, and first this one, already written but inevitably recurring: richness. De Régnier is the rich poet *par excellence*—rich in images. He has coffers full of them, caves full of them, vaults full of them, and unendingly a file of slaves bring him opulent baskets which he disdainfully empties on the dazzling steps of his marble stairs, rainbow-hued cascades that go gushingly, then peacefully to form pools and illuminated lakes. All are not new. To the fittest and fairest metaphors that came before, Verhaeren prefers those he himself creates, though awkward and formless. De Régnier does not disdain metaphors that came before, but he refashions them and converts them to his own use by modifying their setting, imposing new proximities on them, meanings still unknown. If among these reworked images some of virgin matter are found, the impression such poetry gives will none the less be altogether original. In working thus, the bizarre and the obscure are avoided; the reader is not rudely thrown into a labyrinthine forest; he recovers his path, and his joy in gathering new flowers is doubled by the joy of gathering familiar ones.

> Le temps triste a fleuri ses heures en fleurs mortes,
> L'An qui passe a jauni ses jours en feuilles sèches.
> L'Aube pâle s'est vue à des eaux mornes
> Et les faces du soir ont saigné sous les flèches
> Du vent mystérieux qui rit et qui sanglote.

> Melancholy time has ornamented its hours like dead flowers;
> the passing year has yellowed its days like dry leaves.
> The pale dawn is seen by gloomy waters
> and the faces of evening have bled under the arrows
> of the laughing, bleeding, mysterious wind.

Such a poetry certainly charms.

De Régnier in verse can tell everything he wishes, his subtlety is infinite; he notes indefinable nuances of dreams, imperceptible apparitions, fugitive decorations. A naked hand, slightly shriveled, that leans upon a marble table; fruit that swings in the wind and drops; an abandoned pool—such nothings suffice, and the poem springs forth, perfect and pure. His verse is very evocative; in several syllables he forces his vision on us.

> Je sais de tristes eaux en qui meurent les soirs;
> Des fleurs que nul n'y cueille y tombent une à une . . .

> I know sad waters in which die the evenings;
> flowers which nobody gathers fall there one by one.

Different again in this from Verhaeren, he is absolute master of his language. Whether his poems are the result of long or brief labor, they bear no mark of effort, and it is not without amazement, nor even without admiration, that we follow the straight, noble progress of his fair verses, white ambling nags harnessed in gold that sinks into the glory of evenings.

Rich and fine, de Régnier's poetry is never purely lyrical; he encloses an idea in the engarlanded circle of his metaphors, and no matter how vague or general this idea may be, it suffices to strengthen the necklace; the pearls are held by a thread, invisible sometime, but always solid, as in these few verses:

> L'Aube fut si pâle hier
> Sur les doux prés et sur les prêles,
> Qu'au matin clair
> Un enfant vint parmi les herbes,
> Penchant sur elles
> Ses mains pures qui y cueillaient des asphodèles.

> The dawn was so pale yesterday
> over the peaceful meadows and shavegrass;
> and in the clear morning
> came a child to gather plants,
> leaning on them
> his hands were pure that gathered the asphodels.

> Midi fut lourd d'orage et morne de soleil
> Au jardin mort de gloire en son sommeil
> Léthargique de fleurs et d'arbres,
> L'eau était dure à l'oeil comme du marbre,
> Le marbre tiède et clair comme de l'eau,

> Noon was heavy with storm and mournful with sunlight
> in the garden dead of pride in its lethargic sleep
> of flowers and trees;
> the water was hard to the eye like marble,
> the marble warm and clear like water,

Et l'enfant qui vint était beau,
Vêtu de pourpre et lauré d'or,
Et longtemps on voyait de tige en tige encor,
Une à une, saigner les pivoines leur sang
De pétales au passage du bel Enfant.

> and the child that came was comely,
> clad in purple and golden-hair,
> and long one saw the peonies,
> one by one, draw their blood
> from the petals at the passage of the fair child.

L'Enfant qui vint ce soir était nu,
Il cueillait des roses dans l'ombre,
Il sanglotait d'être venu,
Il reculait devant son ombre,
C'est en lui nu
Que mon Destin s'est reconnu.

> The child that came that evening was naked.
> He gathered roses in the dusk,
> he sobbed at having come,
> he retreated before his shadow.
> It is like him, naked,
> that my destiny has recognized itself.

Simple episode of a longer poem, itself a fragment of a book, this little triptych has several meanings and tells different things as one leaves it in its place or isolates it; here, an image of a particular destiny; there, a general image of life, while yet again, one may there see an example of free verse truly perfect and shaped by a master.

FRANCIS VIELÉ-GRIFFIN

I do not wish to say that Vïelé-Griffin is a joyous poet; nevertheless, he is the poet of joy. With him, we share the pleasures of a normal, simple life, the certitude of beauty, the invincible youthfulness of nature. He is neither violent, sumptuous nor sweet: he is calm. Though very subjective, or because of this, for to think of oneself is to think of oneself completely, he is religious. Like Emerson he is bound to see "images of the most ancient religion" in nature, and to think, again like Emerson: "It seems that a day has not been entirely profane, in which some attention has been given to the things of nature." One by one he knows and loves the elements of the forest, from the "great gentle ash trees" to the "million young plants," and it is his very own forest, his personal and original forest:

> Sous ma forêt de Mai fleure tout chèvrefeuille,
> Le soleil goutte en or par l'ombre grasse,
> Un chevreuil bruit dans les feuilles qu'il cueille,
> La brise en la frise des bouleaux passe,
> De feuille en feuille.

> Goat's leaf grows under my May forest.
> The sun drops in gold through the heavy gloom.
> A roe-buck stirs in the leaves he gathers.
> The breeze in the frieze of birches passes
> from leaf to leaf.

> Par ma plaine de mai toute herbe s'argente,
> Le soleil y luit comme au jeu des épées,
> Une abeille vibre aux muguets de la sente
> Des hautes fleurs vers le ru groupées.
> La brise en la frise des frênes chante . . .

> The grasses are silvered in my May field.
> There the sun gleams like a play of swords.
> A bee vibrates to the lilies of the valley in the lane
> of tall grouped flowers, towards the bed of the stream.
> The breeze sings in the frieze of the ash-trees.

But he knows other flowers than those which are common to glades; he knows the flower-that-sings, she who sings, lavendar, sweet marjoram or fay, in the old garden of ballads and tales. The popular songs have left refrains in his memory which he blends in little poems, and which are their commentary or fancy:

Où est la Marguerite,
O gué, ô gué,
Où est la Marguerite?
Elle est dans son château, coeur las et fatigué,
Elle est dans son hameau, coeur enfantile et gai,
Elle est dans son tombeau, semons-y du muguet,
O gué, la Marguerite.

> Where is the Marguerite,
> O gué, o gué,
> where is the Marguerite?
> She is in her château, weary and tired at heart,
> She is in her hamlet, gay and childish at heart.
> She is in her grave, let us gather there the lily-of-the-valley,
> O gué, the Marguerite.

And this is almost as pure as Gerard de Nerval's *Cydalises*:

Où sont nos amoureuses?
Elles sont su tombeau;
Elles sont plus heureuses
Dans un séjour plus beau . . .

> Where are our beloved ones?
> They are in the grave;
> they are happier
> in a fairer sojourn.

And almost as innocently cruel as this round which the little girls sing and dance to:

La beauté, a quoi sert-elle?
Elle sert à aller en terre,
Être mangée par les vers,
Être mangée par les vers . . .

> Of what use is beauty?
> Its use is to go in earth,
> to be eaten by worms,
> to be eaten by worms . . .

Vielé-Griffin has used the popular poetry discreetly—that poetry of such little art that it seems increate—but he would have been less discreet had he misused it, for he has the sentiment and respect for it. Other poets, unfortunately, have been less prudent and have collected the rose-that-talks with such clumsy or rough hands that we wish an eternal silence had been conjured around a treasure now sullied and vilified.

Like the forest, the sea enchants and intoxicates Vielé-Griffin; he has called it all things in his earliest verses, that already remote *Cueille d'Avril*; the insatiable devouring sea, abyss and tomb, the savage sea with triumphal haughty swell, the sea wantoning after voluptuous voids, the furious sea, the heedless sea, the stubborn, dumb sea, the envious sea painting its face with stars or suns, dawns or midnights—and the poet reproaches it for its flown glory:

Ne sens-tu pas en toi l'opulence de n'être
Que pour toi seule belle, ô Mer, et d'être toi?

Do you not feel in you the opulence of being
only for yourself beautiful, O Sea, and of being yourself?

then he proclaims his pride at not having followed the sea's example, at not having sued glory with happy reminiscences or bold plagiarisms. It must be recognized that Vielé-Griffin, who before did not lie, has since kept his word. He has indeed remained himself, truly free, truly proud and truly wild. His forest is not limitless, but it is not a banal forest, it is a domain. I do not speak of the very important part he has had in the difficult conquest of free verse; my impression is more general and deeper and concerns itself not only with the form, but with the essence of his art. Through Francis Vielé-Griffin there is something new in French poetry.

STÉPHANE MALLARMÉ

With Verlaine, Stéphane Mallarmé is the poet who has had the most direct influence on the poets of today. Both were Parnassians and first Baudelairians.

Per me si va tra la perduta gente.

Through me the way that runs among the Lost.

With them one descends along the gloomy mountain to the doleful city of *Fleurs du Mal*. All the present literature and especially that which is called symbolistic, is Baudelairian, not doubtless by its external technique, but by its internal and spiritual technique, by the sense of mystery, by the anxious care to hear what things say, by the desire to harmonize, from soul to soul, with the obscure thought diffused in the night of the world, according to those so often quoted and repeated verses:

La nature est un temple où de vivants piliers
Laissent parfois sortir de confuses paroles;
L'homme y passe à travers des forêts de symboles
Qui l'observent avec des regards familiers.

Nature is a temple where living pillars sometimes
let confused words issue;
man passes there through forests of symbols
watching him with friendly gaze.

Comme de longs échos qui de loin se confondent
Dans une ténébreuse et profonde unité,
Vaste comme la nuit et comme la clarté,
Les parfums, les couleurs et les sons se répondent.

Like long echoes blended
in distance to deep, dim unity,
vast as night and clear as day,
the perfumes, colours and sounds answer each other.

Baudelaire had read the first poems of Mallarmé before dying. He was troubled; poets do not like to leave a brother or son behind them. They would like to be alone and have their genius perish with their brain. But Mallarmé was Baudelairian only by filiation. His so precious originality quickly asserted itself. His *Proses*, his *Après-midi d'un Faune*, his *Sonnets*, came, at too long intervals, to tell of the marvelous subtlety of his patient, disdainful, imperiously gentle genius. Having voluntarily killed in him the spontaneity of being impressionable, the gifts of the artist by degrees replaced the gifts of the poet. He loved words more for their possible sense than for their true sense, and combined them in mosaics of a refined simplicity. It has been well said of him that, like Perseus or Martial, he was a difficult author. Yes, and like Anderson's man who wove invisible threads, Mallarmé assembles gems coloured by his dreams, whose richness our care does not always succeed in divining. But it would be absurd to suppose that he is incomprehensible. The trick of quoting certain verses, obscure by their isolation, is not loyal, for, even in fragments, Mallarmé's poetry, when good, is incomparably so, and if later in a corroded book we only find these debris:

> La chair est triste, hélas! et j'ai lu tous les livres.
> Fuir! là-bas fuir! Je sens que des oiseaux sont ivres
> D'être parmi l'écume inconnue et les cieux . . .

> The flesh is sad, alas! and I have read all the books.
> To fly yonder! I feel that the birds are drunk
> At being among the unknown foam and the heavens . . .

> Un automne jonché de taches de rousseur . . .
> Et tu fis la blancheur sanglotante des lys . . .
> Je t'apporte l'enfant d'une nuit d'Idumée . . .
> Tout son col secouera cette blanche agonie . . .

> An autumn strewn with stains of redness . . .
> And you were the sobbing whiteness of lilies . . .
> I bring you the child of an Idumean night . . .
> His neck will shake off this white agony . . .

we must attribute them to a poet who was an artist to the highest degree. Oh! that sonnet of the swan (of which the last verse quoted above is the ninth) where all the words are white as snow!

But everything possible has been written on this beloved poet. I end with this comment. Recently a question, something like this, was asked:

> Who, in the admiration of the young poets, will replace
> Verlaine, who had replaced Leconte de Lisle?

Few of those questioned answered. Two-thirds of those who abstained were influenced by the ridiculous appearance of such an ultimatum. How in short could it be that a young poet should admire, "exclusively and successively," three "masters" so different as those two and Mallarmé—incontestably chosen? Thus, many were silent because of scruples—but I now vote, saying: Greatly loving and admiring Stéphane Mallarmé, I do not see that Verlaine's death is a decent reason for loving and admiring him more today than yesterday.

Nevertheless, since it is a strict duty ever to sacrifice the dead to the living and to give the living, by an increase of glory, an increase of energy, the result of the vote pleases me, and we, who were silent, would have been bound to speak. What a pity if too much abstention had perverted the truth! For, informed by a circular, the press in this item has found a motive the more for laughing and pitying us, as long as, riding on the inky waves of the sea of intellectual night, but subduer of shipwreckers, the name of Mallarmé, at last written on the ironic elegance of a racing cutter, sails and now defies the emptiness and the bitter-sweet foam of the hoax.

ALBERT SAMAIN

When they know by heart what is pure in Verlaine, the young women of today and tomorrow set out to dream *Au Jardin de l'Infante*. With all that he owes to the author of *Fêtes Galantes* (he owes him less than one might suppose), Albert Samain is one of the most original and charming poets, the sweetest and most delicate of poets:

> En robe héliotrope, et sa pensée au doigts,
> Le rêve passe, la ceinture dénouée,
> Frôlant les âmes de sa traîne de nuée,
> Au rhytme éteint d'une musique d'autrefois . . .

> > In a heliotrope robe, and her thought on her fingers,
> > The dream passes, with loosened girdle,
> > lightly grazing souls with her cloud train,
> > to the extinct rhythm of a music of other times.

One must read the whole little poem which commences thus:

> Dans la lente douceur d'un soir des derniers jours . . .

> > In the lingering fragrance of an evening of the last days.

It is pure and beautiful as any poem in the French language, and its art has the simplicity of works deeply felt and long pondered over. Free verse, new poetry! Here are verses which make us understand the vanity of prosodists and the awkwardness of the too clever players on the zither. A soul is there.

Samain's sincerity is wonderful. I think he would be ashamed to give variations on sensations unexplored by his experience. Sincerity here does not mean candor, nor simplicity gaucherie. He is sincere, not because he avows all his thoughts, but because he thinks of all his avowals. And he is simple because he has studied his art until he knows its last secrets and effortlessly gives forth these secrets with an unconscious mastery:

> Les roses du couchant s'effeuillent sur le fleuve;
> Et, dans l'émotion pâle du soir tombant,
> S'évoque un parc d'automne où rêve sur un banc
> Ma jeunesse déjà grave comme une veuve....

> > The roses of the west shed their leaves on the stream;
> > and, in the pale emotion of the falling evening,
> > is evoked an autumnal park where, on a bench,
> > dreams my youth, already sober as a widow.

This is, it seems, like a Vigny made tender and consenting to the humility of a melancholy quite simple and stripped of scarves.

He is not only softened. He is tender, and what passion and sensuality, but so delicate!

Tu marchais chaste dans la robe de ton âme,
Que le désir suivait comme un faune dompté,
Je respirais parmi le soir, ô pureté,
Mon rêve enveloppé dans tes voiles de femme.

Chastely you walked in the robe of your soul,
which desire followed like a tamed faun;
I breathed through the evening, O purity,
my dream enveloped in your womanly veils.

A delicate sensuality, which is really the impression his verses should give to conform to his poetics, where he dreams

De vers blonds où le sens fluide se délie
Comme sous l'eau la chevelure d'Ophélie,

Fair verses where the fluid sense is loosened
like the hair of Ophelia under the water.

De vers silencieux, et sans rythme et sans trame,
Où la rime sans bruit glisse comme une rame,

Silent verses, without rhythm or trammels,
where the rhyme noiselessly slips like an oar.

De vers d'une ancienne étoffe exténuée,
Impalpable comme le son et la nuée,

Verses of an old thin stuff,
impalpable as sound or cloud.

De vers de soirs d'automne ensorcelant les heures
Au rite féminin des syllabes mineures,

Verses of autumnal evenings bewitching the hours
with the feminine rite of minor syllables.

De vers de soirs d'amours énervés de verveine,
Où l'âme sente, exquise, une caresse à peine....

Verses of evenings of loves enervated with verbena,
where, exquisitely, the soul hardly feels a caress.

But, this poet who would only love nuance, Verlainian nuance, could on some occasions be a violent colourist or a vigorous hewer of marble. This other Samain, older and not less genuine, is revealed in parts of his collection called *Evocations*. It is a Parnassian Samain, but always personal, even in grandiloquence. The two sonnets entitled *Cléopâtre* have a beauty not only of expression but of ideas; it is neither pure music nor pure plastic art. The poem is complete and alive, a strange, disconcerting marble; yes, a living marble whose life stirs and fertilizes the very desert sands, around the momentarily enamoured Sphinx.

Such is this poet: powerfully delicious in the art of making all the bells and all the souls vibrate in harmony. All souls are in love with this "child in robes of state."

PIERRE QUILLARD

I t was in the already far-off and perhaps heroic times of the Art Theatre; we were brought to hear and see *la Fille aux Mains coupées*: To me there remains a most pleasant, complete and perfect memory of a play that truly gave the exquisite and keen sensation of the definitive. That hardly endured an hour; of it remains verses which makes a poem with difficulty forgotten.

Pierre Quillard has reunited his early poetic writings under a title which for more than one will be presumptuous: *La Gloire du Verbe*. To dare this, is to be sure of oneself; to have the consciousness of mastery; to affirm, more or less, that coming after Leconte de Lisle and De Heredia, one will not flag in a craft demanding, along with splendour of imagination, a singular sureness of hand. He has not lied; a very skillful setter, he truly glorifies the multiple jewels of the word. He makes the water of pearls smile and the rainbow of decomposed diamonds laugh.

Captain of a galley filled with precious; slaves, he sails among the tempting perils of purple archipelagos (as the Greek isles are said to appear at certain hours), and when the night comes he seeks the sandy shore of a violet gulf,

> Dans la splendeur des clairs de lune violets.

> In the splendour of violet moonlights.

And he stays for the divine apparition:

> Alors des profondeurs et des ténèbres saintes
> Comme un jeune soleil sort des gouffres marins,
> Blanche, laissant couler des épaules aux reins
> Ses cheveux où nageaient de pâles hyacinthes,
> Une femme surgit . . .

> Then from the depths and holy night,
> as a young sun springs from abysms of the sea,
> white, letting stream from shoulders
> to back her hair where pale hyacinths swim,
> a woman rises.

whose eyes are gulfs of joy, love and terror, and where one sees reflected the whole world of things from grass to the infinity of seas. And she speaks: "Poet who, amidst life, exhibits astonishments and desires and loves, you appear moved by sensual joys and you suffer, for these joys you feel are truly vain, but

Si tu n'étreins que des chimères, si tu bois
L'enivrement de vins illusoires, qu'importe!
Le soleil meurt, la foule imaginaire est morte
Mais le monde subsiste en ta seule âme: vois!
Les jours se sont fanées comme des roses brèves,
Mais ton Verbe a créé le mirage où tu vis....

If you clasp only chimerae, if you drink
the intoxication of delusive wine, what matter!
The sun dies, the imaginary crowd is dead,
but the world subsists in your own soul: See!
the days are faded like brief roses,
but your word has created the mirage in which you live.

and my beauty, you give it form and gesture; I am your creation, I exist because you think of me and because you evoke me."

Such is the leading idea of that *Gloire du Verbe*, one of the rare poems of that time, where the idea and word march in harmonious rhythm.

At sunrise the galley again set sail: Pierre Quillard departed for distant countries.

His is a pagan soul, or which would like to be pagan, for if his eyes eagerly seek sensible beauty, his dream lingers, wishing to force the portal behind which sleeps the beauty enclosed in things. He is truly the more disturbed that he deigns not to mention it, and the glance of the captives disturbs him with more than a shudder. As he knows all the théogonies and all literatures,

J'ai connu tous les dieux du ciel et de la terre,

I have known all the gods of earth and heaven.

as he has drunk at all sources, he knows more than one way to get intoxicated: dilettante of a superior kind, when he will have worn out the joy of sailing, when he will have chosen his residence (doubtless near an old, holy fountain), having collected much, having sown many noble seeds, he will see himself master of a royal garden and of a people odorous with flowers,

Fleurs éternelles, fleurs égales aux dieux!

Eternal flowers, flowers equal to the gods!

A. FERDINAND HEROLD

The danger of free verse is that it remains amorphous, that its rhythm, too little accentuated, gives it some of the characteristics of prose. The finest verse truly remains, it seems to me, the verse formed of a regular number of full or accented syllables and in which the position of the accents is evident and not left to the choice of the reader or declaimer; not only poets read verse, and it is imprudent to place reliance on the chance of interpretations. One rightly supposes that I would not amuse myself by quoting such verses as seemed to me wretched; and above all I would not go to seek them in the poems of Herold, to whom the preference would be unmerited. Not that Herold possesses the gift of rhythm to a high point, but he has it sufficiently to give his poetry the grace of a living thing, sweetly and languidly living. He is a poet of gentleness; his poetry is blond, with pearls in its blond, pure hair, and necklaces and rings, elegant, fine gems, on neck and fingers. This word is the beloved word of the poet; his heroines are flowered with gems as much as his gardens are flowered with lillies.

La blonde, la blanche, la belle Dames des Lys.

The fair, the white, the lovely lady of lilies.

He loved her, but what others, what queens and saints! Reader of forgotten books, he finds precious legends there which he transposes to short poems, often of a sonnet's length. He alone knows these queens, Marozie, Anfelize, Bazine, Paryze, Orable or Aelis, and those saints, Nonita, Bertilla, Richardis—Gemma! She is the first he has thought of; her he gives the most attractive place in the stained glass window, happy again to write that word whose charm he feels.

Herold is one of the most objective of the new poets; he hardly tells of himself; he requires themes that are foreign to his life, and he even chooses those that seem foreign to his beliefs: his queens are not less charming for that, nor his saints less pure. One finds these panels and church windows in the collection entitled *Chevaleries sentimentales,* the most important and most characteristic of his works. It is a truly pleasant reading and one passes sweet hours among those ladies, lilies, gems, and autumn roses.

Les roses d'automne s'étiolent,
Les roses qui fleurissaient les tombes;
Lentement s'effeuillent les corolles
Et le sol froid est jonché de pétales qui tombent.

The autumn roses wither,
the flowers that bedecked the graves;
slowly the corollae are scattered
and the cold ground is strewn with falling petals.

Has not this a quite gentle melancholy? And this:

Il y a des maisons qui pleurent sur le port,
Il y a des glas qui sonnent dans les clochers,
Où tintent des cloches vagues:
Vers quels fleuves de mort
Les vierges ont-elles marché,
Les vierges qui avaient aux doigts de blondes bagues?

There are houses whose fronts weep,
there are knells that toll in the belfry,
where faint bells ring.
Towards what streams of death
have the virgins marched,
the virgins with fair rings on their fingers?

Thus, without forcing his talent to an impassioned expression of life, an effort at which he doubtless would be unskillful, without laying claim to gifts he lacks, Herold has created for his pleasure a poetry of grace, purity, tenderness and sweetness.

If we demanded everything of the same poet, who would answer? The essential thing is to have a garden, to work there with the spade and sow seeds; the flowers that will shoot forth, carnations, peonies or violets, will have their value and their charm, according to the hour and the season.

ADOLPH RETTÉ

By its fecundity in poets, the day we live in and which has already lasted ten years, can hardly be compared with any of the vanished days, even those richest in sunshine and flowers. There were fair morning excursions in the dew, following the footsteps of Ronsard; there was a lovely afternoon when Theophile's weary viol sighed, heard between the oboes and the bass-trombones; there was the stormy romantic day, sombre and royal, interrupted towards evening by the cry of a woman whom Baudelaire was strangling; there was the Parnassian moonlight, and the Verlainian sun rose—and we are there in full noon, in the midst of a wide country provided with everything necessary for the making of verse: plants, flowers, streams, rivulets, woods, caves and young women so fresh that one would say their thoughts were newly hatched from an ingenuous brain.

The wide country is quite full of poets who walk, no longer in troops as in Ronsard's time, but alone and with a slightly sullen air; they greet each other from afar with brief gestures. Not all have names and several of them never will have any. How shall we call them? Let them play on while this person overtakes us and tells us something of his dream.

He is Adolphe Retté.

He is recognizable among them all by his dissolute and almost wild appearance. He crushes the flowers, if he does not gather them, and with reeds he makes rafts, throwing them to the tide, towards peril, towards the morrow. But he smiles and grows languid when young girls pass. *Une belle dame passa* . . . and he spoke:

> Dame des lys amoureux et pâmés,
> Dames des lys languissants et fanés,
> Triste aux yeux de belladone—

> Lady of amourous, swooning lilies,
> Lady of languishing, faded lilies,
> Sad with eyes of belladonna.

> Dame d'un rêve de roses royales,
> Dame des sombres roses nuptiales,
> Frêle comme une madone—

> Lady of dreams of royal roses,
> Lady of sombre, nuptial roses,
> Frail as a madonna—

> Dame de ciel et de ravissement,
> Dame d'extase et de renoncement,
> Chaste étoile très lointaine—

> Lady of heaven and rapture,
> Lady of ecstacy and renouncement,
> Chaste far-away star.

Dame d'enfer, ton sourire farouche,
Dame du diable, un baiser de ta bouche,
C'est le feu des mauvaises fontaines
Et je brûle si je te touche.

> Lady of hell, your sullen smile,
> Lady of the devil, a kiss of your mouth,
> Is the fire of evil fountains,
> And I burn if I touch you.

The fair lady passed, but without being affected by the final imprecation, which she doubtless attributed to excess of love. She passed, giving the poet smile for smile.
This idyll had an admirable plaint for its first epilogue,

Mon âme, il me semble que vous êtes un jardin ...

> My soul, it seems to me, you are a garden ...

a garden where one sees, hanging on the hedges, in the evening mist, shreds of the veil

De la Dame qui est passée.

> Of the lady that has passed away.

Sometime after this adventure, we learned that Retté, returned from a voyage to the *Archipel en fleurs*, had enriched himself with a new collection of dreams. He will yet again enrich himself. His talent is a living shoot grafted on a stout wild stock of glorious viridity. A poet, Adolphe Retté has only the sense of rhythm and the passion for words. He loves ideas and he loves them when they are new and even excessive. He wishes to be freed of all the old prejudices and he would equally like to free his brothers in social bondage. His last books, *la Forêt bruissante* and *Similitudes*, affirm this tendency. The one is a lyrical poem; the other, a dramatic poem in prose, very simple, very curious and very extraordinary by the mixture there seen of the sweet dreams of a tender poet and the somewhat rigid and naive fancies of the Utopian anarchist. But without naivete, that is to say, without freshness of soul, would poets exist?

Some take pleasure, an awkward testimony of a piously troubled admiration, in saying and even in basing a paradoxical study on the saying: "Villiers de L'Isle-Adam was neither of his country nor time." This seems preposterous, for a superior man, a great writer is, in fine, by his very genius, one of the syntheses of his race and epoch, the representative of a momentary humanity, the brain and mouth of a whole tribe and not a fugitive monster. Like Chateaubriand, his brother in race and fame, Villiers was the man of the moment, and of a solemn moment. Both, with differing views and under diverse appearances, recreated the soul of the choice spirits of a period; from one arose romantic Catholicism and that respect for the old traditional stones; and from the other, the idealistic dream and that cult of antique interior beauty. But the one was yet the proud ancestor of our savage individualism; and the other taught us that the life around is the only clay to be shaped. Villiers belonged to his time to such a degree that all his masterpieces are dreams solidly based on science and modern metaphysics, like *l'Ève Future* or *Tribulat Bonhomet*, that enormous, admirable and tragic piece of buffoonery, where all the gifts of the dreamer, ironist and philosopher come to converge, so as to form perhaps the most original creation of the century.

This point cleared, we declare that Villiers, being of prodigious complexity, naturally lends himself to contradictory interpretations. He was everything, a new Goethe, but if less conscious and less perfect, keener, more artful, more mysterious, more human, and more familiar. He is always among us and in us, by his work and by the influence of his work, which exultantly goes through the best of the writers and artists of the actual hour. He has reopened the gates of the beyond, closed with what a crash we remember, and through these gates a whole generation was hurled to infinity. The ecclesiastic hierarchy numbers among her clerks, by the side of the exorcists, the porters, they who must open the door of the sanctuary to all the well-intentioned. Villiers exercised these two functions for us: he was the exorcist of the real arid the porter of the ideal.

Complex, but we may see a double spirit in him. There were two essentially dissimilar writers in him, the romanticist and the ironist. The romanticist was the first to come to birth and the last to die: *Elen* and *Morgane; Akedysseril* and *Axel.* Villiers, the ironist, author of *Tribulat Bonhomet*, is intermediate between these two romantic phases; *l'Ève future* should be described as a mixture of these two so diverse elements, for the book with its overwhelming irony is also a book of love.

Villiers at once realized himself by fancy and irony, making his fancy ironic, when life disgusted him even with fancy. No one has been more subjective. His characters are created with particles of his soul, raised, in the same way as a mystery, to the state of authentic, complete souls. If it is a dialogue, he will cause a certain character to utter philosophies quite above his normal understanding of things. In *Axel*, the abbess speaks of hell as Villiers might have spoken of Hegelianism, whose deceptions he learned towards the end, after having accepted its large certitudes in the beginning: "It is done! the child already experiences the ravishment and intoxications of Hell!" He experienced them: as a Baudelairian, he loved blasphemy for its occult effects, the immense risk of a pleasure taken at the expense of God himself. Sacrilege is in acts, blasphemy in words. He believed in words more than in realities, which are but the tangible shadows of words, for it is quite evident, and by a very simple syllogism, that if there is no thought in the absence of words, no more is there matter in the absence of thought. He believed in the power of words to the point of superstition. The only visible corrections of the second over the first text of Axel, for example, consist in the adjunction of words of a special ending, as when, to evoke an ecclesiastic and conventual society, he uses *proditoire, prémonitoire, satisfactoire,* and *fruition, collaudation,* etc. This very sense of the mystic powers of syllabic articulation stimulates him towards the quest of names as strange as *le Desservant de l'office des Morts,* a church function which never existed unless at the monastery of Saint Apollodora; or *l'Homme-qui-marche-sous-terre,* a name no Indian carried outside of the scenes of the *Nouveau-Monde.*

In a very old rough draft of a page belonging perhaps to *l'Ève future* he has thus defined the *real:*

> Now I say that the Real has its degrees of being. A thing is so much more or less real for us as it interests us more or less, since a thing that interested us not at all would for us be as if it were not—that is to say, much less, though physical, than an unreal thing that interested us.
>
> The Real for us, then, is only what touches the senses or the mind; and according to the degree of intensity with which this sole *real,* which we can judge and name, affects us, we class in our mind the degree of being more or less rich in content as it seems to strike us, and it is consequentlyy legitimate to say that it is realized.
>
> The *idea* is the only control we have of *reality.*

Again:

> And on the top of a distant pine, solitary in the midst of a far-off glade, I heard the nightingale—unique voice of that silence . . .
>
> 'Poetic' landscapes almost invariably leave me quite cold, seeing that for every serious man the most suggestive medium for ideas really poetic is no other than four walls, a table and silence. Those who do not carry within them the soul of everything the world can show them, will do well to watch it: they will not recognize it, each thing being beautiful only according to the thought of him who gazes at it and reflects it in himself. Faith is essential in poetry as in religion, and faith has no need of seeing with corporeal eyes to contemplate that which it recognizes much better in itself . . .

Such ideas were many times, under multiple forms, always new, expressed by Villiers de L'Isle-Adam in his works. Without going as far as Berkeley's pure negations, which nevertheless are but the extreme logic of subjective idealism, he admitted in his conception of life, on the same plan, the Interior and the Exterior, Spirit and Matter, with a very visible tendency to give the first term domination over the second. For him the idea of *progress* was never anything but a subject for jest, together with the nonsense of the humanitarian positivists who teach, reversed mythology, that terrestrial paradise, a superstition if we assign it the past, becomes the sole legitimate hope if we place it in the future.

On the contrary, he makes a protagonist (Edison doubtless) say in a short fragment of an old manuscript of *l'Ève future:*

We are in the ripe age of Humanity, that is all I Soon will come
the senility and decrepitude of this strange polyp, and the
evolution accomplished, his mortal return to the mysterious
laboratory where all the Ghosts eternally work their
experiments, by grace of *some unquestionable necessity*.

And in this last word, Villiers mocks his belief in God. Was he Christian? He became one
towards the end of his life: thus he knew all the forms of intellectual intoxication.

LAURENT TAILHADE

Individualism, which in literature gives us such agreeable baskets of new flowers, often finds itself made sterile by the introduction of the evil weeds of arrogance. One sees young persons, quite puffed up with a monstrous infatuation, declare their intention, not only to produce their work, but at the same the Work, to produce the unique flower, after which the exhausted intelligence must cease being fecund and collect itself in the slow dim task of the reorganization of strength. Even in Paris there are two or three "machines of glory" which have arrogated to themselves alone the right to pronounce this word, which they have banished from the dictionary. That matters little, for the spirit blows where it lists, and when it blows under the skin of frogs and makes them huge, it is for its own amusement, for the world is sad.

Tailhade has none of the grotesque defects of pride; no one has more simply pursued a more simple craft, that of the man of letters. The Romans used a word "rhetorician", and this signified he who speaks, subdues words and subjects them to the yoke of thought; he governs, prompts and stimulates them to the point of imposing, in the very hour of his imaginative work, the hardest, newest, and most dangerous of tasks. Latin by race and tastes, Tailhade has the right to this fine name of rhetorician at which the incompetence of pedants takes offence. He is a rhetorician like Petronius, master equally in prose and poetry.

Here, taken from the rare *Domain de Sonnets*, is one of them:

HÉLÈNE

(Le laboratoire de Faust à Wittemberg)

(Faust's laboratory at Wittenberg)

Des âges évolus j'ai remonté le fleuve,
Et le coeur enivré de sublimes desseins,
Déserté le Hadès et les ombrages saints,
Où l'âme d'une paix ineffable s'abreuve.

> From the evolved ages I have reascended the stream
> and, with a heart intoxicated by sublime designs,
> deserted the Hades and holy shades
> where the soul is steeped in an ineffable calm.

Le Temps n'a pu fléchir la courbe de mes seins.
Je suis toujours debout et forte dans l'épreuve,
Moi, l'éternelle vierge et l'éternelle veuve,
Gloire d'Hellas, parmi la guerre aux noirs tocsins.

> Time has not bent the curve of my breasts.
> I am ever up and strong in trial,
> I, the eternal virgin and eternal widow,
> glory of Hellas, among war with its black tocsins.

O Faust, je viens à toi, quittant le sein des Mères!
Pour toi, j'abandonnai, sur l'aile des chimères,
L'ombre pâle où les dieux gisent, ensevelis.

> O Faust! I come to you, abandoning the bosom of the Mothers!
> For you I have left, on wings of the chimerae,
> the pale shades where he buried the gods.

J'apporte à ton amour, de fond des deux antiques,
Ma gorge dont le Temps n'a pas vaincu les lys
Et ma voix assouplie aux rythmes prophétiques.

> I bring for your love, from the depths of antique skies,
> my neck whose lilies time has not vanquished
> and my voice made supple with prophetic rhythms.

Having written this and *Vitraux*, poems which a disdainful mysticism oddly seasons, and that *Terre latine*, prose of such affecting beauty, perfect and unique pages of an almost sorrowful purity of style, Tailhade suddenly made himself famed and feared by the cruel and excessive satires which he called, as a souvenir and witness of a voyage we all make without profit, *Au pays du Mufle*. The ignominy of the age exasperates the Latin, charmed with sunshine and perfumes, lovely phrases and comely gestures, and for whom money is the joy we throw, like flowers, under the steps of women and not the productive seed which we bury that it may sprout. There he reveals himself the haughty executioner of hypocricies and greeds, of false glories and real turpitudes, of money and success, of the parvenu of the Bourse and the parvenu of *the feuilleton*. Harshly and even unjustly he lashes his own aversions. For him, as for all the satirists, the particular enemy becomes the public enemy, but what beautiful language at once traditional and new, and what grand insolence!

Ce que j'écris n'est pas pour ces charognes!

No more are Tailhade's ballads destined to make dream the handsome ladies who fan themselves with peacock plumes. It is difficult to quote even one of the verses. This one is not very bad:

Bourget, Maupassant et Loti,
Se trouvent dans toutes les gares
On les offre avec le rôti,
Bourget, Maupassant et Loti.
De ces auteurs soyez loti
En même temps que de cigares:
Bourget, Maupassant et Loti
Se trouvent dans toutes les gares.

> Bourget, Maupassant and Loti
> are found in all the stations,
> offered with the roast.
> Bourget, Maupassant
> Choose these authors
> at the same time as the cigars.
> Bourget, Maupassant
> are found in all the stations.

The *Quatorzain d'Été* can be given in full and it is even good to know it by heart, for it is a marvel of subtlety and a little genre picture to care for and preserve. The epigraph, that verse of Rimbaud, in the *Premières Communions,*

> Elle fait la victime et la petite épouse,

> She is the victim and the little spouse.

gives the tone of the frame:

> Certes, monsieur Benoist approuve les gens qui
> Ont lu Voltaire et sont aux Jésuites adverses.
> Il pense. Il est idoine aux longues controverses,
> Il adsperne le moine et le thériaki.

> Truly, Monsieur Benoist approves of persons who
> have read Voltaire and are opposed to Jesuits.
> He muses. He is partial to long controversies,
> calmuniates priest and theriac.

> Même il fut orateur d'une loge écossaise.
> Toutefois—car sa légitime croit en Dieu—
> La Petite Benoist, voiles blancs, ruban bleu,
> Communia. Ca fait qu'on boit maint litre à seize.

> He even was an orator at a Scotch lodge.
> Nevertheless—because his lawful child believes in God—
> his little daughter, in white veils and blue ribbon,
> received communion. This required that several liters at
> sixteen sous be drunk

> Chez le bistro, parmi les bancs empouacrés,
> Le billard somnolent et les garçons vautrés,
> Rougit la pucelette aux gants de filoselle.

> At the *bistro,* among the filthy benches,
> where the billiard man was sleeping, the waiters sprawling,
> and where his little maid in floss-silk gloves was blushing.

> Or, Benoist, qui s'émèche et tourne au calotin,
> Montre quelque plaisir d'avoir vu, ce matin.
> L'hymen du Fils unique et de sa demoiselle.

> Now, Benoist who colours at the sight of a churchman,
> shows some pleasure at having seen, that morning,
> the marriage of the only son and his young girl.

So, with much less wit, Sidonius Appollinaris scoffed the Barbarians among whom the unkindness of the times forced him to live, and like the Bishop of Clermont, it is not in vain that Laurent Tailhade scoffs and chaffs them, for his epigrams will pass beyond the actual time. Meanwhile, I regard him as one of the most authentic glories of the present French letters.

JULES RENARD

Man rises early and walks through deserted roads and lanes; he fears neither dew nor brambles, nor the action of the branches of hedges. He gazes, listens, smells, pursues the birds, the wind, flowers, images. Without haste, but nevertheless anxiously, for she has a delicate ear, he seeks nature, whom he would surprise in her refuge; he finds her, she is there; then, the twigs gently brushed away, he contemplates her in the blue shadow of her retreat and, without having wakened her, closing the curtain, he returns to his home. Before falling asleep, he counts his images: "gently they are reborn at the beck of memory."

Jules Renard has given himself this name: the hunter of images. He is a singularly fortunate and privileged hunter, for alone among his colleagues, he only captures, beasts or little creatures, unpublished prey. He scorns the known, or knows it not; his collection is only of the rare and even unique heads, but which he is in no trouble to put under lock, for they belong to him in such wise that a thief would purloin them in vain. So penetrating and attested a personality has something disconcerting, irritating and, according to some envious persons, extravagant. "Do then as we do, take the old accumulated metaphors from the common treasury; we go swiftly and it is very convenient." But Jules Renard disbelieves in going swiftly. Though unusually industrious, he produces little, and especially little at a time, like those patient engravers who carve steel with geologic slowness.

When studying a writer, one loves (it is an inveterate habit bequeathed us by Sainte-Beuve) to discern his spiritual family, enumerate his ancestors, establish learned connections, and note, at the very least, the souvenirs of long readings, traces of influence and the mark of the hand placed an instant on the shoulder. To whoever has traveled much among books and ideas, this task is simple enough and often easy to the point that it is necessary rather to refrain from it, not to vex the ingenious arrangement of acquired originalities. I have not had this scruple with Renard, but have wished to draw a sketch book; but the odd animal is shown alone, and the leaves only contain, among the arabesques, empty medallions.

To be begotten quite alone, to owe his mind only to himself, to write (since it is a question of writing) with the certitude of achieving the true new wine, of an unexpected, original and inimitable flavor, that is what must be, to the author of *l'Écornifleur* a legitimate motive of joy and a very weighty reason for being less troubled than others about posthumous reputation. Already, his *Poil-de-Carotte*, that so curious type of the intelligent, artful, fatalistic child, has entered into the very form of speech. The "Poil-de-Carotte, you must shut the hens in each evening" equals the most famous words of the celebrated comedies in burlesque truth, and he is at once Cyrano and Molière and will not be robbed of this claim.

Originality being undeniably established, other merits of Jules Renard are distinctness, precision, freshness; his pictures of life, Parisian or rural, have the appearance of dry-point work, occasionally a little thin, but well circumscribed, clear and alive. Certain fragments, more shaded off and ample, are marvels of art, as for instance, *Une Famille d'Arbres*.

It is after having traversed a sun-parched plain that I meet them.

Because of the noise, they do not stand by the road's edge. They inhabit the unploughed fields, near a fountain, like lone birds.

From afar they seem inscrutable. When I approach, their trunks relax. They discreetly welcome me. I can repose and refresh myself, but I divine that they observe and mistrust me.

They live together, the oldest in the center, and the little ones, whose first leaves have just appeared, almost everywhere, without ever dispersing.

They take long to die, and they protect the standing dead until they fall to dust.

They caress each other with their long branches to be assured that they are all there, like the blind. They gesticulate with rage, if the wind puts itself out of breath trying to uproot them. But among themselves, no dispute. They only murmur agreement.

I feel that they should be my real family. I will forget the other. These trees by degrees will adopt me, and to merit this, I understand what must be known.

Already I know how to gaze at passing clouds.

I know, too, how to rest in a spot.

And I almost know how to be silent.

When the anthologies will hail this page, they will hardly have an irony so fine and a poetry so true.

LOUIS DUMUR

To be the representative of logic among an assembly of poets is a difficult role and has its inconveniences. There is the risk of being taken too seriously and consequently of feeling bound to treat literature in grave tones. Gravity is not necessary for the expression of what we believe is truth; irony agreeably seasons the moral decoction; pepper is needed in this camomile. Scornfully to affirm is a sure enough way of not being the dupe of even one's own affirmations. This is practicable in literature, for here all is uncertain and art itself doubtless is but a game where we philosophically deceive each other. That is why it is good to smile.

Louis Dumur rarely smiles. But if, having now gained more indulgence and some rights to real bitterness, he wished to smile so as to excuse and amuse himself, it seems that the whole assembly of poets would protest, astonished and perhaps scandalized. So, by habit and logic, he remains grave.

He is logic itself. He can observe, combine, deduce; his novels, dramas, poems are of a solid construction whose balanced architecture delights by the skillful symmetry of curves, everything directed towards a central dome whither the eye is severely drawn. He is clever and strong enough, when charmed with error, not to abandon it except after having driven it to a corner, with its extremest consequences, and sufficiently master of himself not to confess his error, but even to defend it with all the ingenuities of argument. Such is his system of French verse based on tonic accent; it is true that the result, often deficient, for languages themselves have a quite imperious logic, was occasionally felicitous and unexpected, with hexameters like this.

L'orgueilleuse paresse des nuits, des parfums et des seins.

The proud indolence of nights, perfumes and breasts.

It is towards the theater that Dumur seems definitely to have turned his intellectual activity. The first pages of his plays cut (I do not speak of *Rembrandt*, a purely dramatic history, in the grand style and with vast unfolding), and one is surprised by a renovated setting, retouched words, and a light of conventional realism, an arrangement of things and beings under a new cloak and fresh varnish—but as we go on, the author affirms that in this sad scenic landscape, valid speech will be heard and that a puff of wind turning to tempest will ruin the planting.

The screen, with its new cloth, is so arranged that, its banality destroyed by degrees, beings and things stripped by a caprice of lightning, nothing is left standing but the idea, naked or veiled in its sole, essential mysteriousness.

This old-new setting, then, is the simplest and most available, where the neutral imagination of a throng of eyewitnesses can, with the least effort, place a mental combat whose arms are the accessories of the theater.

A man journeys through the world bearing with him a coffer that contains free natal earth; he carries his love. But a day falls when he is crushed by his love. In the hour of this catastrophe, another man understands, he takes from him the woman who is breaking his arms. To love is to saddle oneself with an imperious burden up to the very moment when, ceasing to be free, one ceases to be strong. *La Motte de terre* explains this lucidly and forcefully. It is the work of a writer thoroughly master of his natural gifts, shaping them with an ease and that air of domination which easily subdues ideas. It happens that a work may be superior to the man and to his very intelligence, but by very little. Though it be little and an innocent untruth, it is a humiliating spectacle and provokes scorn more than the written avowal of the most frightful and complete mediocrity in the brain that gave it birth. The man of worth is always superior to his creation, for his desire is too vast ever to be filled, his love too miraculous ever to be met.

La Nébuleuse is a poem of lovely and deep perspective, where, symbolized by artless beings, are seen the successive generations of men following each other uncomprehendingly, almost undiscerningly, so different are their souls, and always summed up, to the moment of their decline, by the child, the future, the "nebula," whose birth, finally confirmed, brings death, under its morning clearness, to the faded smiles of the aged stars. And, the vision ended, it is urged that this morrow, which is becoming today, will be altogether like its dead brothers, and that in short there is nothing new in the spectacle which amuses the dead years leaning

Sur les balcons du Ciel en robes surannées.

On Heaven's balconies in antiquated robes.

But this "nothingness" has no importance for the human atoms that form and determine it; it is the delightful newness that we breathe and of which we live. The new! The new! And let each intelligence, though short-lived, affirm his will to exist, and to be dissimilar to all antecedent or surrounding manifestations, and let each nebula aspire to the character of a star whose light shall be distinct and clear among other lights.

All this I have read in the text and in the silences of the dialogue, for when the work of art is the development of an idea, the very spaces between lines answer whoever can question them.

Dumur is disposed to create a philosophical theater, a theater of ideas, and also to renew the *roman à these*, for *Pauline ou la Liberté de l'amour* is a serious work, arranged with skill, thought out in an original manner and implying a rare intellectual worth.

GEORGES EEKHOUD

There are few dramatists among the newcomers, I mean fervent observers of the human drama, endowed with that large sympathy which urges the writer to fraternize with all modes and forms of life. To some the people's actions seem unimportant, perhaps because they lack that spirit of philosophic generalization which elevates the humblest happenings to the height of a tragedy. Others have and confess the tendency to simplify everything. They observe and compare facts only to extract summaries and quintessences from them; they have qualms and shame at narrating the mechanisms so often described: they set up soul portraits, keeping of physical anatomy only the materiality necessary to hold the play of colours. Such an art, beside having the disadvantage of being disliked by the reading public (which desires that it be told stories, and which demands it of the newcomer) is the sign of an evident and too disdainful absence of passion. But the dramatist is an impassioned being, a mad lover of life and of the present life, not the things of yesterday, dead representations whose faded decorations are recognizable in lead coffins, but beings of today with all their beauty and animal grossness, their mysterious souls, their true blood that will flow from a heart and not from a swollen bladder, if stabbed in the fifth act.

Georges Eekhoud is a dramatist, a passionate soul, a quaffer of life and of blood.

His sympathies are multifarious and diverse; he loves everything.

"Nourish thyself with all that has life."

Obeying the biblical word, he gathers strength from all the repasts the world offers him, he assimilates the tender or the harsh wildness of peasants or sailors with as much sureness as the most deliberate and hypocritical psychology of creatures drunk with civilization, the disquieting infamy of eccentric loves and the nobility of consecrated passions, the brutal sport of clumsy popular customs and the delicate perversion of certain adolescent souls. He makes no choice, but understands everything because he loves everything.

Nevertheless, whether voluntarily or whether fixed to the natal soil by social necessities, he has limited the field of his fantastic pursuits to the very limits of old Flanders. This agrees marvelously with his genius, which is Flemish, excessive in his sentimental raptures as in his debauches, Phillippe de Champaigne or Jordaens, drawing out lean faces dramatized by the eyes of the fixed idea or displaying all the red irruptions of joyous flesh. Eekhoud, then, is a representative writer of a race, or of a moment of this race. This is important to assure permanence to a work, and a place in the literary histories.

Cycle patibulaire and *Mes communions* seem the two books of Eekhoud where this impassioned man cries his charities, angers, compassions, scorns and loves most clearly and loudly, he himself the third book of that marvelous trilogy whose two first have for title, Maeterlinck and Verhaeren.

Playing a little on the word, I have called him "dramatist," in defiance of the etymologies and usages, although he has never written for the theater; but we divine a genius essentially dramatic by the way in which his narratives are planned and as though miraculously balanced to the sudden changes, the return to their true nature of characters maddened by passion.

He has the genius for sudden changes. A character: then life presses down and the character bends; a new weight straightens and sets him up according to his original truth. It is the very essence of psychological drama, and if the setting shares in the human modifications, the work assumes an air of finality and plenitude, giving an impression of unforseen art by the accepted logic of natural simplicities. This might be a system of composition (not however deficient), but not here: the whisperings of the instinct are hearkened to and welcomed; the necessity of the catastrophe is thrust upon this lucid mind (who has not dulled his mirror by breathing upon it), and he clearly relates the consequences of the seismic movement of the human soul. There are good examples of this art in the tales of Balzac: *El Verdugo* is only a succession of sudden changes, but too concise: Eekhoud's *le Coq Rouge*, just as dramatic, has a much deeper analysis and then is unveiled with grandeur, like a lovely land-scape' effortlessly transformed by the play of clouds and the luminous space.

Equally grand, though with a cruel beauty, is the tragic story simply called *Une mauvaise rencontre* where is seen the heroic transfiguration of the piteous soul of a weak vagrant, overpowered by the strength of a gesture of love and, under the imperious magnetism of the word, blossomed martyr, a stream of pure blood rushing miraculously from the putrefied veins of the social carrion. Later on Mauxgraves enjoys and dies of the terror of having beheld his words realized to their very supreme convulsion, and the red cravat of the predestined become the steel garrote which cuts the white neck in two.

In a novel of Balzac is a rapid, confused episode, which will recall this tragedy to genealogists of ideas. Through hatred of humanity, M. de Grandville has given a note for a thousand francs to a ragpicker, so as to turn him into a drunkard, an idler, a thief; when he returns to his home, he learns that his natural son has just been arrested for theft; it is only romantic. This same anecdote, minus the conclusion, is found in *A Rebours* where des Esseintes acts, but on a young blackguard, nearly like M. de Grandville and through a motive of malignant scepticism. Here is a possible tree of Jesse, but which I declare unauthentic, for the tragic perversity of Eekhoud, chimera or screech-owl, is an original and sincere monster.

If sincerity is a merit, it is doubtless not an absolute literary merit. Art is well pleased with falsehood and no one is particular to confess either his "communions" or his repulsions; but by sincerity I here understand the artistic disinterestedness which acts so that the writer, unafraid of terrifying the average brain or of vexing certain friends or masters, disrobes his thought with the calm wantonness of the extreme innocence of perfect vice—or of passion. Eekhoud's "communions" are impassioned; he eagerly sits down to table and having nourished himself on charity, anger, pity and scorn, having tasted all the love elixirs piously formed by his hate, he rises, drunks but not fed, with the future joys.

PAUL ADAM

The author of *Mystère des Foules* strongly recalls Balzac; he has his power and dispersive force. Like Balzac, but to a much smaller extent, he wrote, while very young, execrable books where no one could have forseen the future genius of an intelligence truly cyclical; *la Force du mal* is no more in the germ in *le Thé chez Miranda* than *le Pere Goriot* in *Jane la Pâle* or *le Vicaire des Ardennes*. Paul Adam, nevertheless, is a precocious person, but there are limits to precocity especially in a writer destined to narrate life exactly as he sees and feels it. It was needful that the education of the senses should have had time to mature and that experience should have fortified the mind in the art of comparisons and choice, the association and disassociation of ideas. A novelist still needs a large erudition and all kinds of ideas that are solidly acquired, but slowly and by chance, by the good will of things and the favorableness of events.

Today Paul Adam is in all his radiance and on the very eve of glory. Each of his gestures, each pace of his brings him nearer to the bomb-ketch ready to explode, and if he withstands the qualing from the thunderclap, he will be king and master. By this bomb-ketch, I do not mean the great mob, but that large public, already selected, which, insensible to pure art, nevertheless demands that its romantic emotions be served enrobed in true literary style, original, strongly perfumed, of long dough cleverly kneaded, and in a form new enough to surprise and charm. This was Balzac's public; it is the public which Paul Adam seems on the point of reconquering. The novel of maimers (I omit three or four masters whom I have not to judge here) is fallen lower than ever since the century and a half when it was brought from England. Neglecting observation, style, imagination and especially ideas, which were rather general than particular, the fictionists who took up the trade of telling stories, have brought fiction to such a point of disrepute that an intelligent man, mindful of employing his leisure in a manner worthy of his intelligence, no longer dares open one of these books, which even the quay book-stalls rebel against and dam up against the yellow current. Paul Adam certainly has suffered through this convulsion of scorn: the lettered men and women, badly informed, have long supposed that his books were like all the rest. They are different.

First by style: Paul Adam uses a language that is vigorous, concise, full of images; new to the point of inaugurating syntactic forms. By observation: his keen glance pierces like a wasp sting through things and souls; like the new photography, he reads through skins and caskets. By the imagination, which permits him to evoke and vivify the most diverse, characteristic and personal beings, he has, like Balzac, the genius not only of giving life to his characters, but personality, of making them true individuals, all well-endowed with an individual soul: in *la Force du Mal*, a young girl is placed so sharply under our eyes that she becomes unforgettable; her character, unfortunately, too abruptly summed up, wavers at the end. By fecundity, finally: fecundity not only linear and of the nature of cleared fields, but of works whose slightest are still works.

He has undertaken two great romantic epopees which his ardent bold spirit will perfect to the condition of monuments, *l'Epoque* and *les Volontés merveilleuses*. He works alone, like a swarm, and at the first ray of sunshine, the bee ideas rush tumultously forth and disperse across the vast fields of life.

Paul Adam is a magnificent spectacle.

LAUTRÉAMONT

He was a young man of savage and unexpected originality, a diseased genius and, quite frankly, a mad genius. Imbeciles grow insane and in their insanity the imbecility remains stagnant or agitated; in the madness of a man of genius some genius often remains: the form and not the quality of the intelligence has been affected; the fruit has been bruised in the fall, but has preserved all its perfume and all the savor of its pulp, hardly too ripe.

Such was the adventure of the amazing stranger, self-adorned with this romantic pseudonym: Comte de Lautréamont. He was born at Montevideo in April, 1846, and died at the age of twenty-eight, having published the *Chants de Maldoror* and *Poésies,* a collection of thoughts and critical notes of a literature less exasperated and even, here and there, too wise. We know nothing of his brief life: he seems to have had no literary connection, the numerous friends apostrophized in his dedications bearing names that have remained secrets.

The *Chants de Maldoror* is a long poem in prose whose six first chants only were written. It is probable that Lautréamont, though living, would not have continued them. We feel, in proportion as we finish the reading of the volume, that consciousness is going, going— and when it returns to him, several months before his death, he composes the *Poésies,* where, among very curious passages, is revealed the state of mind of a dying man who repeats, while disfiguring them in fever, his most distant memories, that is to say, for this infant, the teachings of his professors!

A motive the more why these chants surprise. It was a magnificent, almost inexplicable stroke of genius. Unique this book will remain, and henceforth it remains added to the list of works which, to the exclusion of all classicism, forms the scanty library and the sole literature admissible to those minds, oddly amiss, that are denied the joys, less rare, of common things and conventional morality.

The worth of the *Chants de Maldoror* is not in pure imagination: fierce, demoniac, disordered or exasperated with arrogance in crazy visions, it terrifies rather than charms; then, even in unconsciousness, there are influences that can be determined. "O Nights of Young," the author exclaims in his verses, "what sleep you have cost me!" And here and there he is swayed by the romantic extravagances of such English fictionists as were still read in his time, Anne Radcliffe and Maturin (whom Balzac esteemed), Byron, also by the medical reports on eroticism, and finally by the bible. He certainly had read widely, and the only author he never quotes, Flaubert, must never have been far from his reach.

This worth I would like to make known, consists, I believe, in the novelty and originality of the images and metaphors, by their abundance, the sequence logically arranged like a poem, as in the magnificent description of a shipwreck, where all the verses (although no typographie artifice betokens them) end thus: "The ship in distress fires cannon shots of alarm; but it founders slowly . . . majestically." So, too, the litanies of the Ancient Ocean:

> Ancient Ocean, your waters are bitter. I greet you, Ancient
> Ocean. Ancient Ocean, O great celibate, when you course the
> solemn solitudes of your phlegmatic realms . . . I greet you,
> Ancient Ocean.

Here are other images: "like a corner, as far as the eye can reach, where shivering cranes deliberate much, and soar sturdily in winter athwart the silence."

And this terrifying invocation: "silk-eyed octopus." To describe men he uses expressions of a Homeric suggestiveness: narrow-shouldered men, ugly-headed men, lousy-haired men, the man with pupils of jasper, red-shanked men. Others have a violence magnificently obscene:

> He returns to his terrified attitude and continues to watch, with a nervous trembling, the male hunt, and the great lips of the vagina of gloom, whence ceaselessly flow, like a river, immense dark spermatazoae which take their flight in the desolate ether, concealing entire nature with the vast unfolding of their bat wings, and the solitary legions of octopuses, saturnine and doleful at watching these hollow inexpressible fulgurations.

(1868: so that one cannot class them as phrases fancied from some print of Odilon Redon). But what a theme, on the other hand, what a story for the master of retrograde forms, of fear and the amorphous stirrings of beings that are near—and what a book, written, we might say, to tempt him!

Here is a passage, at once quite characteristic of Lautréamont's talent and of his mental malady:

> With slow steps the brother of the blood-sucker (Maldoror) marched through the forest . . . Then he cried: "Man, when you come upon a dead dog, pressed against a milldam so as to prevent it from issuing, go not like the others, and take with your hands the worms that flow from his swollen belly, considering it with astonishment, opening a knife, and then cutting a great number of them from the body, as you repeat that you too will be no more than this dog. What mystery seek you? Neither I nor the four fins of the sea bear of the Northern Seas have succeeded in solving the problem of life . . . Who is this being, near the horizon, that fearlessly approaches, with troubled oblique bounds? And what majesty blended with serene gentleness! His gaze, though kind, is piercing. His enormous eyelids play with the breeze and appear alive. He is unknown to me. My body trembles as he fixes his monstrous eyes on me. Something like a dazzling aureole of light plays around him . . . How fair he is . . . You should be powerful, for you have a form more than human, sad as the universe, beautiful as suicide . . . How! . . . it is you, toad! . . . great toad . . . unfortunate toad! . . . Pardon! . . . What do you on this earth where are the accursed? But what have you done with your viscous fetid pustules to have such a sweet air? I saw you when you descended from above, poor toad! I was thinking of infinity, and at the same time of my weakness . . . Since then you have appeared to me monarch of the ponds and marshes! Covered with a glory which belongs only to God, you have departed thence, leaving me consoled, but my staggering reason founders before such grandeur . . . Fold your white wings and gaze not from on high with those troubled eyes."

The toad rests on its hind legs (which resemble those of a man) and, while the slugs, woodles, and snails flee at the sight of their mortal enemy, gives utterance to those words:

"Hearken, Maldoror. Notice my figure, calm as a mirror . . . I am but a simple dweller of the reeds, 'tis true, but thanks to your own contact, taking of good only what is in yourself, my reason has grown and I can converse with you . . . As for myself, I should prefer to have protruding eyes, my body lacking feet and hands, to have killed a man, than to be as you are. For I hate you! Adieu, then, hope not to find again the toad in your passage. You have been the cause of my death. I leave for eternity, to implore pardon for you."

Alienists, had they studied this book, would have classified the author among those aspiring to pass for persecuted persons: in the world he only sees himself and God—and God thwarts him. But we might also inquire whether Lautréamont is not a superior ironist, a man forced by a precious scorn for mankind to feign a madness whose incoherence is wiser and more beautiful than the average reason. There is the madness of pride; there is the delirium of mediocrity. How many balanced and honest pages, of good and clear literature, would I not give for this, for these words and phrases under which he seems to have wished to inter reason herself! The following is taken from the singular *Poésies*:

The perturbations, anxieties, depravations, deaths, exceptions in the physical or moral order, spirit of negation, brutishness, hallucinations fostered by the will, torments, destruction, confusions, tears, insatiabilities, servitudes, delving imaginations, novels, the unexpected, the forbidden, the chemical singularities of the mysterious vulture which lies in wait for the carrion of some dead illusion, precocious and abortive experiences, the darkness of the mailed bug, the terrible monomania of pride, the innoculation of deep stupor, funeral orations, desires, betrayals, tyrannies, impieties, irritations, acrimonies, aggressive insults, madness, temper, reasoned terrors, strange inquietudes which the reader would prefer not to experience, cants, nervous disorders, bleeding ordeals that drive logic at bay, exaggerations, the absence of sincerity, bores, platitudes, the somber, the lugubrious, childbirths worse than murders, passions, romancers at the Courts of Assize, tragedies, odes, melodramas, extremes forever presented, reason hissed at with impunity, odour of hens steeped in water, nausea, frogs, devil-fish, sharks, simoom of the deserts, that which is somnambulistic, squint-eyed, nocturnal, somniferous, noctambulistic, viscous, equivocal, consumptive, spasmodic, aphrodisiac, anaemic, one-eyed, hermaphroditic, bastard, albino, pédéraste, phenomena of the aquarium and the bearded woman, hours surfeited with gloomy discouragement, fantasies, acrimonies, monsters, demoralizing syllogisms, ordure, that which does not think like a child, desolation, the intellectual manchineel trees, perfumed cankers, stalks of the camelias, the guilt of a writer rolling down the slope of nothingness and scorning himself with joyous cries, remorse, hypocrisies, vague vistas that grind one in their imperceptible gearing, the serious spittles on inviolate maxims, vermin and their insinuating titillations, stupid prefaces like those of Cromwell, Mademoiselle de Maupin and Dumas *fils*, decaying, helplessness, blasphemies, suffocation, stifling, mania—before these unclean charnel houses, which I blush to name, it is at last time to react against whatever disgusts us and bows us down.

Maldoror (or Lautréamont) seems to have judged himself in making himself apostrophised thus by his enigmatic Toad: "Your spirit is so diseased that it perceives nothing; and you deem it natural each time there issues from your mouth words that are senseless, though full of an infernal grandeur."

TRISTAN CORBIÈRE

Laforge, in the course of a reading, sketched some notes regarding Corbière which, though not printed, are nevertheless definitive, as for instance:

> Bohemian of the Ocean—picaresque and tramp—breaking down, concise, driving his verse with a whip—strident as the cry of gulls, and like them never wearied—without aestheticism—nothing of poetry or verse, hardly of literature— sensual, he never reveals the flesh—a blackguard and Byronic creature—alway the crisp word—there is not another artist in verse more freed of poetic language—he has a trade without plastic interest—the interest, the effect is in the whip stroke, the dry-point, the pun, the friskiness, the romantic abruptness— he wishes to be indefinable, uncataloguable, to be neither loved nor hated; in short, declassed from every latitude, every custom hither and beyond the Pyrenees.

This doubtless is the truth: Corbière all his life was dominated and led by the demon of contradiction. He supposed that one must be differentiated from men by thoughts and acts exactly contrary to the thoughts and acts of the mass of men; there is much of the willful in his originality; he labored at it as women labor over their complexion during long afternoons between sky and earth, and when he disembarked, it was to draw broadsides of stupefaction. Dandyism à la Baudelaire.

But a nature cannot be developed except in the sense of its instincts and inclinations. Corbière had inherently to be something of what he became, the Don Juan of singularity; it is the only woman he loves; he mocks the other with the clever phrase "the eterna madame."

Corbière has much wit, wit at the same time of the Montmartre wine-shop and of the blade of past times. His talent is formed of the braggart spirit, uncouth and humbug, of a bad impudent taste, of genius thrusts. He has the drunken air, but he is only laboriously clumsy; to make absurd chaplets, he shapes from miraculous, rolled pebbles works of a secular patience, but in the dizaine he leaves the little stone of the sea quite naked and rough, because at bottom he loves the sea with a great naiveté and because his folly for paradoxical things gives way, from time to time, to an intoxication of poetry and beauty.

Among the never ordinary verses of *Amours jaunes*, are many that are admirable, but admirable with an air so equivocal, so specious, that we do not always enjoy them at the first meeting; then we judge that Tristan Corbière is, like Laforgue, a little his disciple, one of those undeniable, unclassable talents which are strange and precious exceptions in the history of literature—singular even in a gallery of oddities.

Here are two little poems of Tristan Corbière, forgotten even by the last publisher of the *Amours jaunes*:

PARIS NOCTURNE

C'est la mer;—calme plat—Et la grande marée
Avec un grondement lointain s'est retirée....
Le flot va revenir se roulant dans son bruit.
Entendez-vous gratter les crabes de la nuit.

It is the sea;—calm sheet. And the great tide
with distant rumbling has receded . . .
The wave returns, wallowing in its noise.
Do you hear the clawing of the night crabs.

C'est le Styx asséché: le chiffonier Diogène,
La lanterne à la main, s'en vient avec sans-gêne.
Le long du ruisseau noir, les poètes pervers
Pêchent: leur crâne creux leur sert de boîte à vers.

It is the drained Styx: Diogenes,
lantern in hand, unceremoniously arrives.
Perverse poets angle along the black stream:
their hollow skulls serve as boxes for worms.

C'est le champ: pour glaner les impures charpies
S'abat le vol tournant des hideuses harpies;
Le lapin de gouttière, à l'affût des rongeurs.
Fuit les fils de Bondy, nocturnes vendangeurs.

It is the field: to glean impure lint
falls the whirling flight of hideous harpies;
the gutter rabbit, on the watch for rodents,
flees the sons of Bondy, nocturnal vintagers.

C'est la mort: la police gît.—En haut l'amour
Fait sa sieste, en tétant la viande d'un bras lourd
Où le baiser éteint laisse sa plaque rouge.
L'heure est seule. Écoutez. Pas un rêve ne bouge.

It is death: the policeman lies dead. On high, love
takes a siesta, sucking the meat with heavy hand
where the extinguished kisses leave a red patch.
Alone is the hour. Listen. Not a dream stirs.

C'est la vie: écoutez, la source vive chante
L'éternelle chanson sur la tête gluante
D'un dieu marin tirant ses membres nus et verts
Sur le lit de la Morgue . . . et les yeux grands ouverts.

It is life: listen, the living source sings
the eternal song on the head of
a sea-god drawing green naked limbs
on the bed of the Morgue . . . and the great open eyes.

PARIS DIURNE

Vois aux deux le grand rond de cuivre rouge luire,
Immense casserole où le bon Dieu fait cuire
La manne, l'arlequin, l'éternel plat du jour.
C'est trempé de sueur et c'est trempé d'amour.

> See gleaming in the skies the great disk of red copper,
> immense casserole where the good God cooks
> manna, the harlequin, eternal *plat du jour*.
> It is dipped in sweat and dipped in love.

Les laridons en cercle attendent prés du four,
On entend vaguement la chair rance bruire,
Et les soiffards aussi sont là, tendant leur buire,
Les marmiteux grelotte en attendant son tour.

> The laridons wait in a circle near the oven;
> vaguely one hears the rustling of rancid flesh,
> and the tipplers, too, are there, holding out their jugs;
> the wretches shiver, waiting their turn.

Crois-tu que le soleil frit donc pour tout le monde
Ces gras graillons grouillants qu'un torrent d'or inonde?
Non, le bouillon de chien tombe sur nous du ciel.

> D you think the sun then fries for everybody
> these fat stirring scraps of burnt meat which a flood of gold
> inundates?
> No, the dog-soup falls on us from the sky.

Eux sont sous le rayon et nous sous la gouttière.
A nous le pot au noir qui froidit sans lumière.
Notre substance à nous, c'est notre poche à fiel.

> They are beneath the ray and we beneath the gutter.
> To us the black jug that grows cold without light.
> Our substance for ourselves is our bag of gall.

Born at Morlaix in 1845, Tristan returned there in 1875 to die of inflammation of the lungs. He was the son (others say the nephew) of the sea romancer, Edouard Corbière, author of *Négrier*, whose violent love for the things of the sea had such a strong influence upon the poet. This *Négrier*, by Edouard Corbière, captain on a long-voyage vessel, 1832, 2 vol. in-8, is a quite interesting tale of maritime adventures. The fourth chapter of the first part, entitled *Prisons d'Angleterre*, (the convict ships) contains the most curious details about the habits of the prisoners, about the loves of the *corvettes* with the "*forts-a-bras*"—in one place, the author says, where "there was only one sex." The preface of this novel reveals a spirit that is very proud and very disdainful of the public: the same spirit with some talent and a sharper nervousness—you have Tristan Corbière.

ARTHUR RIMBAUD

Jean Nicolas Arthur Rimbaud was born at Charleville, October 20, 1854, and from the most tender age showed traits of the most insupportable blackguardism. His brief stay in Paris was in 1870-71. He followed Verlaine in England, then in Belgium. After the little misunderstanding which separated them, Rimbaud roved through the world, followed the most diverse trades, a soldier in the army of Holland, ticket taker at Stockholm in the Loisset circus, contractor in the Isle of Cyprus, trader at Harrar, then at Cape Guardafui, in Africa, where a friend of M. Vittorio Pico saw him, applying himself to the fur trade. It is likely that, scorning all that lacks brutal gratification, savage adventure, the violent life, this poet, singular among all, willingly renounced poetry. None of the authentic pieces of *Reliquaire* seem more recent than 1873; although he did not die before the end of 1891. The verses of his extreme youth are weak, but from the age of seventeen Rimbaud acquired originality, and his work will endure, at least by virtue of phenomena. He is often obscure, bizarre and absurd. Of sincerity nothing, with a woman's character, a girl's, inherently wicked and even savage, Rimbaud has that kind of talent which interests without pleasing. In his works are pages which give the impression of beauty one feels before a pustulous toad, a good-looking syphillitic woman, or the Chateau-Rouge at eleven o'clock in the evening. *Les Pauvres à l'èglise, les Premières Communions* possess an uncommon quality of infamy and blasphemy. *Les Assis* and *le Bateau ivre*—there we have the excellent Rimbaud, and I detest neither *Oraison du soir* nor *les Chercheuses de Poux*. He was somebody after all, since genius ennobles even baseness. He was a poet. Some verses of his have remained living almost in the state of ordinary speech:

> Avec l'assentiment des grands héliotropes.

> With the assent of the tall sunflowers.

Some stanzas of *Bateau ivre* belong to true and great poetry:

> Et dès lors je me suis baigné dans le poème
> De la mer, infusé d'astres et latescent,
> Dévorant les azurs verts où, flottaison blême
> Et ravie, un noyé pensif parfois descend,
> Où, teignant tout à coup les bleuités, délires
> Et rythmes lents sous les rutilements du jour,
> Plus fortes que l'alcool, plus vastes que vos lyres,
> Fermentent les rousseurs amères de l'amour.

> And since, then, I have bathed me in the poem
> of the sea, steeped in stars and latescent,
> mastering the green azure where, flotation pale
> and ravished, a pensive drowned person sometimes descends;
> where, suddenly staining the nuances of blue, frenzied
> and slow rhythms beneath the glinting red of day,
> stronger than alcohol, vaster than your lyres,
> the bitter redness of love ferments.

The whole poem marches: all of Rimbaud's poems march, and in *les Illuminations* there are marvelous belly dances.

It is a pity that his life, so poorly known, was not the true *vita abscondita*; what is known disgusts from what can be understood of it. Rimbaud was like those women whom we are not surprised to learn have taken to religion in some house of shame; but what revolts still more is that he seems to have been a jealous and passionate mistress: here the aberration becomes debauched, being sentimental. Senancour, the man who has spoken most freely of love, says of these inharmonious liaisons where the female falls so low that she has no name except in the dirtiest slang:

> When in a very particular situation, the need results in a minute of misconduct, we can perhaps pardon men totally vulgar, or at least banish its memory; but how understand that which becomes a habit, an attachment? The fault may have been accidental; but that which is joined to this act of brutality, that which is not unforseen, becomes ignoble. If even a passion capable of troubling the head and almost of depriving one of liberty, has often left an ineffaceable stain, what disgust will not a consent given in cold-blood inspire? Intimacy in this manner, that is the height of shame, the irremediable infamy.

But the intelligence, conscious or unconscious, though not having all rights, has the right of all absolutions.

> ... Qui sait si le genie
> N'est pas une de vos vertus,

> ... Who knows if genius
> is not one of your virtues,

monsters, whether you are called Rimbaud—or Verlaine?

FRANCIS POICTEVIN

Like all writers who have achieved an understanding of life, Francis Poictevin, though a born novelist, promptly renounced the novel. He knows that everything happens, that a fact in itself is not more interesting than another fact and that the manners of expression alone have significance.

I recall something to this effect reported by Sarcey à propos of the lamentable Murger:

> About gave him a subject for a novel; he made nothing of it. He was decidedly a sluggard." It is very difficult to persuade certain old men—old or young—that there are no *subjects*; there is only a *subject* in literature, and that he who writes, and all literature, that is to say all philosophy, can arise equally from the cry of a run-over dog as from Faust's exclamations as he questions Nature: "Where seize thee, O infinite Nature? And thou, Breasts?

The author of *Tout Bas* and of *Presque,* like any other person, could have arranged his meditations in dialogues, order his sentiments into chapters divided at random, insinuate through pseudo-living characters a bit of gesticulating life and have them express, by the act of kneeling on the flag-stones of some familiar church, the virtue of an unrecognized creed: in short, write "the novel of mysticism" and popularize the practice of mental prayer for the "literary journals." By this means his books would have gained him a popularity which certainly he now lacks, for few writers among those whose talent is evident are so little esteemed, less known and less discussed. Poictevin disdains all artifice save the artifice of style, a snare into which we are content to fall. Whether he notes the delicacies of a flower, a little girl's attitude, the grace of a madonna, or the cold and quite hard purity of Catherine de Gênes, he wins us with sure strokes, by that very preciosity with which some clumsily reproach him. This preciosity is rigorously personal. Apart from all groups, as remote from Huysmans as from Mallarmé, the author of *Tout Bas* works, one would say, in a cell, an ideal cell he carries with him while traveling; and there, standing, often kneeling, he pours out his poems and prayers in phrases that have the unique musical quality of a Byzantine organ. Less phrases than vibrations, vibrations so peculiar that few souls find themselves attuned. Music of Gregorian plain-chant, such as one listens to in a sumptuous Flemish church, with sudden fugues of exalted prayer that soar aloft towards the high lines and hurl themselves against the painted vaults, kindling old stained-glass windows, illuming the lines of the darkened cross with love. The mystic monk, the true mystic, Fra Angelico, and Bonaventura a little, live again in the pages of *Presque* with its chatoyant spirituality, more than in all the pseudo-mystic literature of our time. Would not the author of *Recordare sanctae crucis* find more satisfaction in this prayer than in the patronizing and fructiferous deductions:

> Here below the Christ appears the most adorable, most
> absorbed figure of the eternal substance, scented with all
> virtues; a figure with dulcet blues, the burning clear yellows of
> topaz or chrysanthemum, the blood-red hues of future glories.
> And despite my daily relapses, I compel myself, according to
> Jesus' word to the Samaritan, to adoration in spirit and in
> truth.

Poictevin has entered the "Garden of all the flowerings" of which Saint Bonaventura sang:

> Crux deliciarum hortus
> In quo florent omnia . . .

> Torment of the garden of delight
> In which everything flourishes . . .

and kneeling, he has kissed the heart of roses whose rosary is of blood—the blood of the great
torment. While Morning, fair-haired youth, delivers moist adolescence to folly-driven women,
he goes towards a priestly peace, to masses of solitude, and one of the graces gathered is that
his soul becomes impregnated with the "interior light, *claritas caritas.*"

It is the essential point. Mere phrases, yes; but the phrases are no more than the attire
and reserve of his art. He has felt, dreamed or thought before speaking; especially has he loved:
and some of his, metaphors leap like a fervent prayer, like one of the cries of Saint Theresa.

He strives clearly to reach the bottom, to penetrate even the vital center of the hortensia's
umbel. Everywhere he seeks—and finds—the soul. No one is less a rhetorician than this stylist,
for the rhetorician is he who clothes the solid common things with garments fit to sustain all
the vulgarity of bedizenings, while Poictevin ever diaphanizes a phantom, a rainbow,
an illusion, an azalea flower, thus:

> Would a hand of a consumptive in the contraction of its quasi-
> diaphaneity, leaning, not lazily, but which no longer is
> conscious, seem to warn, less exalted than before and
> indulgently returned?

Yes, how subtle it is!—and why not write "like everybody"?

Alas! that is forbidden him—because he is a mystic, because he feels new rapports between
man and God, and because, veiled in the dolorous perfection of a form where grace becomes
pearled in minutiae, Poictevin is a spontaneous writer. How many things, doubtless, has he
never transcribed, afraid of not having discovered the exact expression, the unique and very
rare, the unedited!

Everything, indeed, in a work of art should be unedited—and even the words, by the
manner of grouping them, of shaping them to new meanings—and one often regrets having
an alphabet familiar to too many half-lettered persons.

Disciple of Goncourt, from whom he further sharpened his precious style of writing,
Francis Poictevin by degrees refined himself to immateriality. And that is just his genius,
the expression of the immaterial and the inexpressible: he invented the mysticism of style.

ANDRÉ GIDE

In 1891 I wrote as follows à propos of the *Cahiers d'André Walter*, an anonymous work:

> The diary is a form of good literature and perhaps the best for some extremely subjective minds. De Maupassant would make nothing of it. For him the world is like the cover of a billiard table; he notes the meetings of the balls and stops when the balls stop, for if there is no further material movement to be perceived, there is nothing more to be said, The subjective soul feeds on itself through the reserve of its stored sensations; and, by an occult chemistry, by unconscious combinations whose numbers approach infinity, those sensations, often of a faraway past time, become changed and are multiplied in ideas. Then are narrated, not anecdotes, but the very anecdotes of oneself, the only kind that can often be retold, if one has the talent and gift to vary their appearances. In this way has the author of these copy books worked and thus will he work again. His is a romantic and philosophic mind, of the lineage of Goethe. One of these years, when he will have recognized the helplessness of thought against the onward course of things, its social uselessness, the scorn it inspires in that mass of corpuscles named society, indignation will seize him, and since action, though illusive, is forever closed to him, he will wake armed with irony. This oddly enough, is a writer's finishing touch; it is the co-efficient of his soul's worth. The theory of the novel, stated in a note of page 120 is of more than mediocre interest; we must hope that the author upon occasion will recollect it. As for the present book, it is ingenuous and delicate, the revealer of a fine intelligence. It seems the condensation of a whole youth of study, dreams and sentiment, of a tortuous, timorous youth. This reflection (p. 142) rather well sums up André Walter's state of mind: 'O, the emotion when one is quite near to happiness, when one has but to touch it—and passes on.'

There is a certain pleasure in not having been deceived in one's first judgment of the first book of an unknown person. Now that André Gide has, after several intelligent works, become one of the most luminous of the Church's Levites, with the flames of intelligence and grace quite visible around his brow and in his eyes, the time nears when bold discoverers will discuss his genius, and, since he fares forth and advances, sound the trumpets of the advancing column. He deserves the glory, if anyone merits it (glory is always unjust) since to the originality of talent the master of minds willed that in this singular being should be joined an originality of soul. It is a gift rare enough to justify speaking of it.

A writer's talent is often nothing but the terrible faculty of retelling, in phrases that seem beautiful, the eternal clamors of mediocre humanity. Even gigantic geniuses, like Victor Hugo or Adam de Saint-Victor were destined to utter an admirable music whose grandeur consists in concealing the immense emptiness of the deserts: their soul is like the formless docile soul of deserts and crowds; they love, think, and desire the loves, thoughts, desires of all men and of all beasts; poets, they magnificently declaim what is not worth the trouble of being thought.

The human species, doubtless, in its entire aspect of a hive or colony, is only superior to the bison species or the king-fisher, because we are a part of it; here and there man is a sorry automaton; but his superiority lies in his ability to attain consciousness; a small number reach this stage. To acquire the full consciousness of self is to know oneself so different from others that one no longer feels allied with men except by purely animal contacts: nevertheless, among souls of this degree, there is an ideal fraternity based on differences—while social fraternity is based on resemblances.

The full consciousness of self can be called originality of soul—and all this is said only to point out the group of rare beings to which André Gide belongs.

The misfortune of these beings, when they wish to express themselves, is that they do it with such odd gestures that men fear to approach them; their life of social contacts must often revolve in the brief circle of ideal fraternities; or, when the mob consents to admit such souls, it is as curiosities or museum objects. Their glory is, finally, to be loved from afar and almost understood, as parchments are seen and read above sealed glass cases.

But all this is related in *Paludes*, a story, as is known, "of animals living in dusky caverns, and which lose their sight through never being used"; it is also, with a more intimate charm than in the *Voyage d' Urien*, the ingenuous story of a very complicated, very intellectual and very original soul.

PIERRE LOUYS

At this moment there is a little movement of neo-paganism, of sensual naturalism and erotism at once mystic and materialistic, a springtime of those purely carnal religions where woman is adored even for the very ugliness of her sex, for by means of metaphors we can idealize the imperfect and deify the illusive. A novel of Marcel Batilliat, a young unknown man, is, despite its serious faults, perhaps the most curious specimen of this erotic religiosity which zealous hearts are cultivating as dreams or ideals. But there is a famous manifestation, the *Aphrodite* of Pierre Louys, whose success, doubtless, henceforth will stifle as under roses, all other claims of sexual romanticism.

It is not, although its appearance has deceived young and old critics, a historical novel, such as *Salammbô* or even *Thaïs*. The perfect knowledge which Pierre Louys possesses of Alexandrian religions and customs has allowed him to clothe his personages with names and garbs veraciously ancient, but the book must be read divested of those precautions which are not there, just as in more than one eighteenth century novel, where the customs, gestures and desires of an incontestable today are at play behind the embroidered screen work of hieratic phallophores.

By the vulgarizing of art, love finally has returned to us naked. It is in the epoch of the flowering of Calvinism that the nude began to be banned from manners and that it sought refuge in art, which alone treasured the tradition of it. Formerly, and even in the time of Charles the Fifth, there were no public celebrations without speculations regarding lovely nude women; the nude was so little dreaded that adulterous women were driven stark naked through the towns. It is beyond a doubt that, in the mysteries, such roles as Adam and Eve were acted by persons free of fleshings—monstrous display. To love the nude, and first of all femininity with its graces and insolences, is traditional in those races which hard reform has not altogether terrorized. The idea of the nude being admitted, costume can be modified to take in floating loose robe, manners can be softened, and something of splendour illume the gloom of our hypocricies. By its vogue, *Aphrodite* has signalled the possible return to manners where there will be a bit of freedom; coming from that period, this book has the value of an antidote.

But how fallacious is such a literature. All these women, all this flesh, the cries, the luxury so animal, so empty and so cruel! The females gnaw at the brains; thought flies horror-stricken; woman's soul oozes away as by the action of rain, and all these copulations engender nothingness, disgust and death.

Pierre Louys has felt that his fleshly book logically must end in death: *Aphrodite* closes in a scene of death, with obsequies.

It is the end of *Atala* (Chateaubriand invisibly hovers over our whole literature), but gracefully refashioned and renewed with art and tenderness—so well that the idea of death comes to join itself with the idea of beauty; the two images, entwined like two courtisans, slowly fades into the night.

Sincerity, what an enormous unreasonable demand, if it is a question of woman! Those most praised for their candor were nevertheless comedians, like the weeping Marceline, an actress moreover who wept through her life, as in a role, with the consciousness which the plaudits of the public give. Since women have written, not one has had the good faith to speak and confess themselves in bold humility, and the only ideas of feminine psychology known to literature must be sought in the literature of men. There is more to learn of women in *Lady Roxanna* than in the complete works of George Sand. It is not perhaps a question of untruthfulness; it is rather a natural incapacity to think for herself, to take cognizance of herself in her own brain, and not in the eyes and in the lips of others; even when they ingenuously write into little secret diaries, women think of the unknown god reading—perhaps—over their shoulders. With a similar nature, a woman, to be placed in the first ranks of men, would require even a higher genius than that of the highest man; that is why, if the conspicuous works of men are often superior to the men themselves, the finest works of women are always inferior to the worth of the women who produced them.

This incapacity is not personal; it is generic and absolute. It is needful, then, to compare women exclusively with themselves, and not scorn them for whatever of egoism or personality is lacking: this fault, outside of literature and art, is generally estimated as equal to a positive virtue.

Whether they essay their charms in perversity or candor, women will better succeed in living than in playing their comedy; they are made for life, for the flesh, for materiality— and they will joyfully realize their most romantic dreams if they do not find themselves arrested by the indifference of man whose more sensitive nerves suffer from vibrating in the void. There is an evident contradiction between art and life; we have hardly ever seen a man live in action and dream at the same time, transposing in writing the gestures that first were real: the equivalence of sensations is certain and the horrors of fear can better be described by whosoever imagines them than by the man that experiences them. On the contrary, the predominance in a temperament of tendencies to live, dulls the sharpness of the imaginative faculties. With the more intelligent women, those best gifted for cerebral pursuits, the impelling motivation will most easily be translated into acts than into art. It is a physiological fact, a state of nature it would be as absurd to reproach women with as to blame men for the smallness of their breasts or the shortness of their hair. Moreover, if it is a question of art, the discussion, which touches such a small number of creatures, has for humanity, like all purely intellectual questions, but an interest of the steeple or the street corner.

All this, then, being admitted, and it also being admitted that *l'Animale* is Rachilde's most singular book (although not the most ambiguous) and that *le Démon de l'Absurde* is the best, I will willingly add, not for the sole pleasure of contradicting myself and destroying the virtue of the preceding pages, that this collection of tales and imaginative dialogue proves to me a realized effort at true artistic sincerity. Pages like *la Panthère* or *les Vendanges de Sodom* show that a woman can have phases of virility, to write, careless of necessary coquetteries or customary attitudes, make art with nothing but an idea and from words, create.

J. K. HUYSMANS

Le Romanée and Chambertin, Clos-Vougeot and Corton made the abbatial pomps, princely fetes, opulences of vestments figured in gold, aglow with light, pass before him. The Clos-Vougeot especially dazzled him. To him that wine seemed the syrup of great dignitaries. The etiquette glittered before his eyes, like glories surrounded by beams, placed in churches, behind the occiput of Virgins.

The writer who in 1881, in the midst of the naturalistic morass, had, before a name read on a wine list, such a vision, although ironic, of evoked splendours, must have puzzled his friends and made them suspect an approaching defection. In fact, several years later, the unexpected *A Rebours* appeared, and it was not a point of departure, but the consecration of a new literature. No longer was it so much a question of forcing a brutal externality to enter the domains of Art by representation, as of drawing from this very representation motives for dreams and interior revaluations. *En Rade* further developed this system whose fruitfulness is limitless—while the naturalistic method proved itself still more sterile than even its enemies had dared hope—a system of strictest logic and of such marvelous suppleness that it permits, without forfeiting anything to likelihood, to intercalate in exact scenes of rustic life, pages like "Esther" or like the "*voyage sélenién.*"

The architecture of *Là-Bas* is based on an analogous plan, but the license profitably finds itself restrained by the unity of subject, which remains absolute beneath its multiple faces: the Christ of Gunewald, in his extreme mystic violence, his startling and consoling hideousness, is not a fugue without line, nor are the demoniac forest of Tiffauges, the cruel Black Mass, or any of the "fragments" displaced or inharmonious; nevertheless, before the freedom of the novel, they had been criticized, not in themselves, but as not rigorously necessary to the advance of the book. Fortunately the novel is finally free, and to say more, the novel, as still conceived by Zola or Bourget, to us appears a conception as superannuated as the epic poem or the tragedy. Only, the old frame is still able to serve; it sometimes is necessary to entice the public to very arduous subjects, to simulate vague romantic intrigues, which the author unravels at his own will, after he has said all he wished to say. But the essential of yesterday is become the accessory, and an accessory more and more scorned: quite rare at the present hour are those writers who are clever or strong enough to confine themselves to a demolished genre, to spur the fatigued cavalry of sentimentalities and adulteries.

Moreover, aesthetics tends to specialization in as many forms as there are talents: among many vanities are admissible arrogances to which we cannot refuse the right to create into normal characters. Huysmans is of those; he no longer writes novels, he makes books, and he plans them according to an original arrangement; I believe that is one of the reasons why some persons still take issue with his literature and find it immoral. This last point is easy to explain by a single word: for the non-artist, art is always immoral. As soon as one wishes, for example, to translate sexual relations into a new language, he is immoral because he discloses, fatally, acts which, treated by ordinary procedures, would remain unperceived, lost in the mist of common things. Thus it is that an artist, not at all erotic, can be accused of stupid outrages by the foolish or the mischievous, before the public.

It, nevertheless, does not seem that the facts of love or rather of aberration related in *Là-Bas* at all entice the simplicity of virginal ignorance. This book rather gives disgust or horror of sensuality in that it does not invite to foolish experiences or even to permissible unions. Will not immorality, if we behold it from a particular and peculiarly religious point of view, consist, on the contrary, in the insistence upon the exquisiteness of carnal love and the vaunting of the delights of legitimate copulation?

The Middle Age knew not: our hypocrisies. It was not at all ignorant of the eternal turpitudes, but it knew how to hate them. It had no use for our conduct, nor for our refinements; it published the vices, sculped them on its cathedral portals and spread them in the verses of its poets. It had less regard for refraining from terrifying the fears of mummied souls than for tearing apart the robes and revealing the man, and showing to man, so as to make him ashamed, all the ugliness of his low animality. But it did not make the brute wallow in his vice; it placed him on his knees and made him lift his head. Huysmans has understood all this, and it was difficult to conquer. After the horrors of the satanic debauch, before the earthly punishment, he has, like the noble weeping people he evokes, forgiven even the most frightful slayers of infants, the basest sadist, the most monstrous fool that ever was.

Having absolved such a man, he could without pharisaism absolve himself, and with the aid of God, some more humble and quite brotherly succor, of helpful reading, visitations to gentle conventual chapels, Huysmans one day found himself converted to mysticism, and wrote *En Route*, that book which is like a statue of stone that suddenly begins to weep. It is a mysticism a little raucous and hard, but like his phrases, his epithets, Huysmans is hard. Mysticism first came to him through the eyes rather than through the soul. He observed religious facts with the fear of being their dupe and the hope that they would be absurd; he was caught in the very meshes of the *credo-quia-absurdum*—happy victim of his curiosity.

Now, fatigued at having watched men's hypocritical faces, he watches the stones, preparing a supreme book on "The Cathedral." There, if it is a question of feeling and understanding, is it especially a question of sight. He will see as no other person has seen, for no one other person has seen, no one ever was gifted with a glance so sharp, so boring, so frank and so skilled in insinuating himself into the very wrinkles of faces, rose-windows and masks.

Huysmans is an eye.

JULES LAFORGUE

In the *Fleurs de bonne Volonté* is a little complaint, like the others, called *Dimanches*:

Le ciel pleut sans but, sans que rien l'émeuve,
Il pleut, il pleut, bergère! sur le fleuve . . .

> The sky rains without ending, though nothing agitates it;
> it rains, it rains, shepherdess! on the stream . . .

Le fleuve a son repos dominical;
Pas un chaland, en amont, en aval.

> The stream has its dominical repose;
> not a barge up stream, downstream.

Les vêpres carillonnent sur la ville,
Les berges sont désertes, sans une île.

> Vespers chime in the town;
> the banks are deserted, not an isle.

Passe un pensionnat, ô pauvres chairs!
Plusieurs out déjà leurs manchons d'hiver.

> Passes a boarding-school group, o poor flesh!
> Several already have on their winter muffs.

Une qui n'a ni manchon ni fourrure
Fait tout en gris une bien pauvre figure;

> One that has neither muff nor fur
> makes a quite sorry figure all in gray.

Et la voilà qui s'échappe des rangs
Et court: ô mon Dieu, qu'est-ce qui lui prend?

> And see! She breaks from the ranks
> and runs; O God, what has seized her?

Elle va se jeter dans le fleuve.
Pas un batelier, pas un chien de Terre-Neuve . . .

> She goes and throws herself in the stream.
> Not a boatman, not a Newfoundland dog . . .

And there we have, prophesized, the sudden absurd death, the life of Laforgue. His heart was too cold; he departed.

His was a mind gifted with all the gifts and rich with important acquisitions. With his natural genius made up of sensibility, irony, imagination and clairvoyance, he had wished to nourish it with positive knowledge, all the philosophies, all the literatures, all the images of nature and art; and even the latest views of science seemed to have been familiar to him. He had an ornate flamboyant genius, ready to construct architectural works infinitely diverse and fair, to rear new ogives and unfamiliar domes; but he had forgotten his winter muff and died one snowy day of cold.

That is why his work, already magnificent, is only the prelude of an oratorio ended in silence.

Many of his verses are as though reddened by a glacial affectation of naiveté; they speak of the too dearly cherished child, of the young girl hearkened to—but a sign of a true need of affection and of a pure gentleness of heart—adolescent of genius who would still have wished to place on the knees of his mother, his "equatorial brow, greenhouse of anomalies." But many have the beauty of purified topazes, the melancholy of opals, the freshness of moon-stones, and some pages, like that which commences thus:

> Noire bise, averse glapissante
> Et fleuve noir, et maisons closes . . .

> Dismal north wind, screaming downpour
> and black stream, and shut houses . . .

have a sad, consoling grace, with eternal avowals: forever on the same subject, Laforgue retells it in such fashion that it seems dreamed and confessed for the first time. And I think that what we must demand of the translator of dreams is, not to wish to fix forever the fugacity of a thought or air, but to sing the song of the present hour with such frank force that it seems the only one we could hear, the only one we could understand. In the end, perhaps, it is necessary to become reasonable and delight us with the present and with new flowers, indifferent, except as a botanist, to the faded fields. Every epoch of thought, art or sentiment should take a deep delight in itself and go down from the world with the egoism and languor of a superb lake which, smiling upon the old streams, receives them, calms them, and absorbs them.

There was no present for Laforgue, except among a group of friends. He died just as his *Moralités Légendaires* was coming to birth, but still offered to a minority, and he had just learned from some mouths that these pages consecrated him to live the life of glory among those whom the gods created in their image, they, too, gods and creators. It is a literature entirely new and disconcertingly unexpected, giving the curious sensation (specially rare) that we have never read anything like it; the grape with all its velvet hues in the morning light, but with curious reflections and an air as if the seeds within had become frozen by a breath of ironic wind come from some place farther than the pole.

On a copy of *l'Imitation de Notre-Dame la Lune*, offered to Bourget (and since thrown among old papers in the quay) Laforgue wrote: "This is only an *inter-mezzo*. I pray you to wait yet awhile, and give me until my next book"—but he was of those who ever look forward to finding themselves in their next work, the noble unsatisfied who have too much to say ever to believe that they have said other things than prolegomenae and prefaces. If his interrupted work is but a preface, it belongs to those which counterbalance a finished work.

JEAN MORÉAS

Raymond de la Tailhède thus exalts Moréas:

Tout un silence d'or vibrant s'est abattu,
Près des sources que des satyres ont troublées,
Claire merveille éclose au profond des vallées,
Si l'oiselet chanteur du bocage s'est tu.

A full silence of vibrant gold has descended
near the springs which satyrs have troubled;
a clear marvel enclosed in the heart of the valleys,
if the little singing bird remains silent.

Oubli de flûte, heures de rêves sans alarmes,
Où tu as su trouver pour ton sang amoureux
La douceur d'habiter un séjour odoreux
De roses dont les dieux sylvains te font des armes

Oblivion of the flute, hours of fearless dreams,
where you have known how to find for your amorous blood
the peacefulness of inhabiting a place odorous
with roses, whose sylvan gods make arms for you.

Là tu vas composant ces beaux livres, honneur
Du langage français et de la noble Athènes.

There you go, composing beautiful books, a credit
to the French language and noble Athens.

These verses are romances, that is, of a poet to whom the romantic period is but a witch's night where unreal sonorous gnomes stir, of a poet (this one has talent) who concentrates his efforts to imitate the Greeks of the Anthology through Ronsard, and to steal from Ronsard the secret of his laborious phrase, his botanical epithets, and his sickly rhythm. As for what is exquisite in Ronsard, since that little has passed into tradition and memory, the Romantic school had to neglect it on pain of quickly losing what alone constitutes its originality. There is I know not what of provincialism, of steps against life's current, of the loiterer, in this care for imitation and restoration. Somewhere Moréas sings praise

De ce Sophocle, honneur de la Ferté-Milon,

Of that Sophocles, credit to Ferté-Milon.

and it is just that: the Romantic school always has the air of coming from Ferté-Milon.

But Jean Moréas, who has met his friends on the road, started from somewhere farther away, introduces himself more proudly.

Arrived in Paris like any other Wallachian or Eastern student, and already full of love for the French language, Moréas betook himself to the school of the old poets and frequented the society of Jacot de Forest and Benoit de Sainte-Maure. He wished to take the road to which every clever youth should vow himself who is ambitious to become a good harper; he swore to accomplish the complete pilgrimage: At this hour, having set out from the *Chanson de Saint-Léger*, he has, it is said, reached the seventeenth century, and this in less than ten years. It is not as discouraging as one supposes. And now that texts are more familiar, the road shortens: from now on less halts. Moréas will camp under the old Hugo oak, and, if he perseveres, we shall see him achieve the aim of his voyage, which doubtless is to catch up with himself. Then, casting aside the staff, often changed and cut from such diverse copses, he will lean on his own genius and we will be able to judge him, if that be our whim, with a certain security.

All that today can be said is that Moréas passionately loves the French language and poetry, and that the two proud-hearted sisters have smiled upon him more than once, satisfied to see near their steps a pilgrim so patient, a cavalier armed with such good-will.

> Cavalcando l'altrjer per un cammino,
> Pensoso dell andar che mi sgradia,
> Trovai Amor in mezzo della via
> In abito legger di pellegrino.

> Once while riding on a journey,
> pensive along the route that displeased me,
> I found love in the middle of the road
> in a vagrant's scant attire.

Thus Moréas goes, quite attentive, quite in love, and in the light robe of a pilgrim. When he called one of his poems *le Pèlerin passionné*, he gave an excellent idea and a very sane symbolism of himself, his role and his playings among us.

There are fine things in that *Pèlerin*, and also in *les Syrtes*; there are admirable and delicious touches and which (for my part) I shall always joyfully reread, in *les Cantilènes*, but inasmuch as Moréas, having changed his manner, repudiates these primitive works, I shall not insist. There remains *Ériphyle*, a delicate collection formed of a poem of four "sylvae", all in the taste of the Renaissance and destined to be the book of examples where the young "Romans", spurred on by the somewhat intemperate invectives of Charles Maurras, must study the classic art of composing facile verses laboriously. Here is a page:

> Astre brillant, Phébé aux ailes étendues,
> O flamme de la nuit qui croîs et diminues,
> Favorise la route et les sombres forêts
> Où mon ami errant porte ses pas discrets!

> Brilliant star, Phoebe with outspread wings,
> O name of night that grows and wanes,
> favor my way through the gloomy forest
> where my errant soul takes its modest steps!

Dans la grotte au vain bruit dont l'entrée est tout lierre,
Sur la roche pointue aux chèvres familière,
Sur le lac, sur l'étang, sur leurs tranquilles eaux,
Sur les bords émaillés où plaignent les roseaux.
Dans le cristal rompu des ruisselets obliques,
Il aime à voir trembler tes feux mélancoliques.

    In the grotto of hollow sound, whose entrance is ivy-covered,
    on the rock topped with the familiar she-goat,
    on the lake, on the pond, on the tranquil waters,
    on the enamelled banks where reeds moan,
    in the crystal broken by oblique rills
    she likes to see the trembling of your melancholy fires.

Phébé, ô Cynthia, dès sa saison première,
Mon ami fut épris de ta belle lumière;
Dans leur cercle observant tes visages divers,
Sous ta douce influence il composait ses vers.
Par dessus Nice, Eryx, Seyre et la sablonneuse
Ioclos, le Tmolus et la grande Epidaure,
Et la verte Cydon, sa piété honore
Ce rocher de Latmos où tu fus amoureuse.

    Phoebe, O Cynthia, from the first season
    my soul was drunk with your lovely light;
    observing your diverse faces in their orb,
    beneath your gentle influence, she composed verses.
    Above Nicias, Eryx, Siris and the sandy Iolchos,
    Timolus and the grand Epidorus,
    and Green Sidon, her piety reveres
    this rock of Latmos where you loved.

Moréas, like his Phoebe, has tried to put on many diverse countenances and even to cover his face with masks. We always recognize him from his brothers: he is a poet.

STUART MERRILL

The logic of an amateur of literature is offended upon his discovering that his admirations disagree with those of the public; but he is not surprised, knowing that there are the elect of the last hour. The public's attitude is less benignant when it learns the disaccord which is noticeable between it, obscure master of glories, and the opinion of the small oligarchic number. Accustomed to couple these two ideas, renown and talent, it shows a repugnance in disjoining them; it does not admit, for it has a secret sense of justice or logic, that an illustrious author might be so by chance alone, or that an unknown author merits recognition. Here is a misunderstanding, doubtless old as the six thousand years ascribed by La Bruyère to human thought, and this misunderstanding, based on very logical and solid reasoning, sets at defiance from the height of its pedestal all attempts at conciliation. To end it, it is needful to limit oneself to the timid insinuations of science and to ask if we truly know the "thing in itself," if there is not a certain inevitable little difference between the object of knowledge and the knowledge of the object. On this ground, as one will be less understood, agreement will be easier and then the legitimate difference of opinions will be voluntarily admitted, since it is not a question of captivating Truth—that reflection of a moon in a well—but to measure by approximation, as is done with stars, the distance or the difference existing between the genius of a poet and the idea we have of it.

Were it necessary, which is quite useless, to express oneself more clearly, it might be said that, according to several persons whose opinion perhaps is worth that of many others, all the literary history, as written by professors according to educational views, is but a mass of judgments nearly all reversed, and that, in particular, the histories of French literature is but the banal cataloguing of the plaudits and crowns fallen to the cleverest or most fortunate. Perhaps it is time to adopt another method and to give, among the celebrated persons, a place to those who could have attained it—if the snow had not fallen on the day they announced the glory of the new spring.

Stuart Merrill and Saint-Pol-Roux are of those whom the snow gainsaid. If the public knows their names less than some others, it is not that they have less merit, it is that they had less good fortune.

The poet of *Fastes*, by the mere choice of this word, bespeaks the fair frankness of a rich soul and a generous talent. His verses, a little gilded, a little clamorous, truly burst forth and peal for the holidays and gorgeous parades, and when the play of sunshine has passed, behold the torches illumined in the night for the sumptuous procession of supernatural women. Poems or women, they doubtless are bedecked with too many rings and rubies and their robes are embroidered with too much gold; they are royal courtisans rather than princesses, but we love their cruel eyes and russet hair.

After such splendid trumpets, the *Petits Poèmes d'Automne*, the noise of the spuming wheel, a sound of a bell, an air of a flute in tone of moonlight: it is the drowsiness and dreaming saddened by the silence of things, the incertitude of the hours:

C'est le vent d'automne dans l'allée,
Soeur, écoute, et la chute sur l'eau
Des feuilles du saule et du bouleau,
Et c'est le givre dans la vallée,

It is the autumn wind in the lane,
sister, listen, and the fall of willow
and beach tree leaves on the water,
and the hoar-frost in the valley.

Dénoue—il est l'heure—tes cheveaux
Plus blonds que le chanvre que tu files . . .

Let down—it is the hour—your hair
fairer than the hemp you spin . . .

Et viens, pareille à ces châtelaines
Dolentes à qui tu fais songer,
Dans le silence où meurt ton léger
Rouet, ô ma soeur des marjolaines!

And come, like those drooping great ladies,
to him who is thinking of you,
in the silence when your light spinning-wheel
dies, O sister of the sweet marjoram.

Thus, in Stuart Merrill we discover the contrast and struggle of a spirited temperament and a very gentle heart, and according as one of the two natures prevails, we hear the violence of brasses or the murmurings of viols. Similarly does his technique oscillate from *Gammes* to his latest poems, from the Parnassian stiffness to the *verso suelto* of the new schools, which only the senators of art do not recognize. Vers libre, which is favorable to original talent, and which is a reef of danger to others, could not help winning over so gifted a poet, and so intelligent an innovator. This is how he understands it:

Venez avec des couronnes de primevères dans vos mains,
O fillettes qui pleurez la soeur morte à l'aurore.
Les cloches de la vallée sonnent la fin d'un sort,
Et l'on voit luire des pelles au soleil du matin.

Come with wreathes of primroses in your hands,
O young girls, who mourn the sister dead at dawn.
Bells of the valley peal the end of a destiny,
and spades are seen gleaming in the morning sun.

Venez avec des corbeilles de violettes, ô fillettes
Qui hésitez un peu dans le chemin des hêtres,
Par crainte des paroles solennelles du prêtre.
Venez, le ciel est tout sonore d'invisibles alouettes . . .

Come with baskets of violets, O young girls
who slightly hesitate in the path of beeches,
for fear of the priest's solemn words.
Come, the sky is quite sonorous with invisible larks . . .

C'est la fête de la mort, et l'on dirait dimanche,
Tant les cloches sonnent, douces au fond de la vallée;
Les garçons se sont cachés dans les petites allées;
Vous seules devez prier au pied de la tombe blanche . . .

      It is the festival of the dead, one would say Sunday,
      the bells ring so gently in the heart of the valley;
      boys have hidden in the lanes;
      you go alone to pray at the foot of the white grave.

Quelque année, les garçons qui se cachent aujourd'hui
Viendront vous dire à toutes la douce douleur d'aimer,
Et l'on vous entendra, autour du mât de mai,
Chanter des rondes d'enfance pour saluer la nuit.

      Some year, the boys, who today are hidden,
      will come to tell you the sweet pain of loving,
      and they will hear you all, around the maypole,
      sing songs of childhood to greet the night.

Stuart Merrill did not embark in vain, the day he desired to cross the Atlantic, to come and woo the proud French poetry, and place one of her flowers in his hair.

One of the most fruitful and astonishing inventors of images and metaphors. To find new expressions, Huysmans materializes the spiritual and the intellectual spheres, thus giving his style a precision somewhat heavy and a lucidity rather unnatural: *rotten souls* (like teeth) and *cracked hearts* (like an old wall); it is picturesque and nothing else. The inverse operation is more conformable to the old taste of men for endowing vague sentiments and a dim consciousness to objects. It remains faithful to the pantheistic and animistic tradition without which neither art nor poetry would be possible. It is the deep source from which all the others are formed, pure water transformed by the slightest ray of sunshine into jewels sparkling like fairy collars. Other "metaphorists" like Jules Renard, venture to seek the image either in a reforming vision, a detail separated from the whole becoming the thing itself, or in a transposition and exaggeration of metaphors in usage; finally, there is the analogic method by which, without our voluntary aid, the meaning of ordinary words change daily. Saint-Pol-Roux blends these methods and makes them all contribute to the manufacture of images which, if they are all new, are not all beautiful. From them a catalogue or a dictionary could be drawn up:

> Wise-Woman of light — the cock.
> Morrow of the caterpillar in balldress   — butterfly.
> Sin that sucks — natural child.
> Living distaff — mutton.
> Fin of the plow — plowshare.
> Wasp with the whip sting — diligence.
> Breast of crystal — flagon.
> Crab of the hand — open hand.
> Letter announcement — magpie.
> Cemetery with wings — a flight of crows.
> Romance for the nostrils — perfume of flowers.
> To tame the carious jawbone of bemol of a modern tarask — to play the piano.
> Surly gewgaw of the doorway — watchdog.
> Blaspheming limousine — wagoner.
> To chant a bronze alexandrine — to peal midnight.
> Cognac of Father Adam — the broad, pure air.
> Imagery only seen with closed eyes — dreams.
> Leaves of living salad — frogs.
> Green chatterers — frogs.
> Sonorous wild-poppy — cock-crow.

The most heedless person, having read this last, will decide that Saint-Pol-Roux is gifted with an imagination and with an equally exuberant wretched taste. If all these images, some of which are ingenious, followed one after another towards *les Reposoirs de la Procession* where the poet guides them, the reading of such a work would be difficult and the smile would often temper the aesthetic emotion; but strewn here and there, they but form stains and do not always break the harmony of richly coloured, ingenious and grave poems. *Le Pèlerinage de Sainte-Anne*, written almost entirely in images, is free of all impurity and the metaphors, as Théophile Gautier would have wished, unfold themselves in profusion, but logically and knit together; it is the type and marvel of the prose poem, with rhythm and assonance.

In the same volume, the *Nocturne* dedicated to Huysmans is but a vain chaplet of incoherent catachreses: the ideas there are devoured by a frightful troop of beasts. But *l'Autopsie de la Vieille fille*, despite a fault of tone, but *Calvaire immémorial*, but *l'Ame saisissable* are masterpieces. Saint-Pol-Roux plays on a zither whose strings sometimes are too tightly drawn: a turn of the key would suffice for our ears ever to be d eeply gladdened.

ROBERT DE MONTESQUIOU

U pon the first appearance of his *Chauves-Souris* in violet velvet, the question was seriously put whether de Montesquiou was a poet or an amateur of poetry, and whether the fashionable world could be harmonized with the cult of the Nine Sisters, or of any one of them, for nine women are a lot. But to discourse in such fashion is to confess one's unfamiliarity with that logical operation called the dissociation of ideas, for it seems elementary logic separately to evaluate the worth or beauty of the tree and its fruit, of man and his works. Whether jewel or pebble, the book will be judged in itself, disregarding the source, the quarry or the stream from which it comes, and the diamond will not change its name, whether hailing from the Cape or from Golconda. To criticism the social life of a poet matters as little as to Polymnia herself, who indifferently welcomes into her circle the peasant Burns and the partician Byron, Villon the purse-snatcher and Frederick II, the king: Art's book of heraldry and that of Hozier are not written in the same style.

So we will not disturb ourselves with unraveling the flax from the distaff, or ascertaining what of illusiveness de Montesquiou and his status of a man of fashion have been able to add to the renown of the poet.

The poet, here, is "a précieuse".

Were those women really so ridiculous, who, to place themselves in the tone of some fine and gallant poets, imagined new ways of speech, and, through a hatred of the common, affected a singularity of mind, costume and gesture? Their crime, after all, was in not wishing to conform with the world, and it seems that they paid dearly for this, they—and the entire French poetry which, for a century and a half, truly feared ridicule too much. Poets at last are freed from such horrors; in fact they are now allowed to avow their originality; far from forbidding them to go naked, criticism encourages them to assume the free easy dress of the gymnosophist. But some of them are tattooed.

And that is really the true quarrel with de Montesquiou: his originality is excessively tattooed. Its beauty recalls, not without melancholy, the complicated figurations with which the old Australian chieftains were wont to ornament themselves; there is even an odd refinement in the nuances, the design, and the amusing audacities of tone and lines. He achieves the arabesque better than the figure, and sensation better than thought. If he thinks, it is through ideographic signs, like the Japanese:

> Poisson, grue, aigle, fleur, bambou qu'un oiseau ploie,
> Tortue, iris, pivoine, anémone et moineaux.

> Fish, crane, eagle, flower, bird-bent bamboo.
> Turtle, iris, peony, anemone, sparrows.

He loves these juxtapositions of words, and when he chooses them, like those above, soft and vivid, the landscape he seeks is quite pleasantly evoked, but often one sees, relieved against an artificial sky, hard unfamiliar forms, processions of carnival larvae— Or rather, women, girls, birds—baubles deformed by a too Oriental fancy; baubles and trinkets:

Je voudrais que ce vers fût un bibelot d'art,

I wish that this verse were a bauble of art,

is the aesthetics of de Montesquiou, but the bauble is no more than an amusing fragile thing to be placed under a glass case or closet—yes, preferably in a closet. Then, disburdened of all this grotto work, all this lacquer, all this delicate paste, and as he himself wittily says, all these "shelves of infusoria," the poet's museum would become an agreeable gallery, where one would pleasantly muse before the many metamorphoses of a soul anxious to give a new nuance-laden grace to beauty. With the half of he *Hortensias bleus* one could make a book, still quite thick, which would be almost entirely composed of fine or proud or delicate poetry. The author of *Ancilla,* of *Mortuis ignotis,* and of *Tables vives* would appear what he truly is, excluding all travesty—a good poet.

Here is a part of the *Tables vives,* whose title is obscure, but whose verses have beautiful clarity, despite the too familiar sound of some too Parnassian rimes and some verbal incertitudes:

Apprenez à l'enfant à prier les flots bleus,
Car c'est le ciel d'en bas dont la nue est l'écume,
Le reflet du soleil qui sur la mer s'allume
Est plus doux à fixer pour nos yeux nébuleux.

Learn from the child to pray to the blue waves,
for it is the sky here below whose cloud is foam.
The sun's reflection sparkling on the sea
is sweeter to gaze on to our gloomy eyes.

Apprenez à l'enfant à prier le ciel pur,
C'est l'océan d'en haut dont la vague est nuage.
L'ombre d'une tempête abondante en naufrage
Pour nos coeurs est moins triste à suivre dans l'azur.

Learn from the child to pray to the pure sky,
it is the ocean above, whose void is cloud.
The gloom of a cloud rich in wrecks
to our hearts is less sad to follow in the azure.

Apprenez à l'enfant à prier toutes choses:
L'abeille de l'esprit compose un miel de jour
Sur les vivants *ave* du rosaire des roses,
Chapelet de parfums aux dizaines d'amour . . .

Learn from the child to pray to all things:
the bee of the spirit makes a honey of light
on the living *aves* of the rosary of roses,
a chaplet of perfumes on the rosaries of love.

In short, de Montesquiou exists: blue hortensia, green rose or white peony, he is of those flowers one curiously gazes upon in a bed of flowers, whose name one asks and whose memory one cherishes.

GUSTAVE KAHN

Domaine De Fée, a Song of Songs recited by one lone voice, very charming and very amorous, in a Verlainian setting—O eternal Verlaine!

> O bel avril épanoui,
> Qu'importe ta chanson franche,
> Tes lilas blancs, tes aubépines et l'or fleuri
> De ton soleil par les branches,
> Si loin de moi la bien-aimée
> Dans les brumes du nord est restée.

> O lovely April, glad and bright,
> what matters your blithe song,
> white lilacs, hawthorns, and the flowered gold
> of sunlight streaming through the branches,
> if far-away my well-beloved
> in the northern fogs stays.

That is the tone. It is very simple, very delicate, very pure and sometimes biblical:

> J'étais allé jusu'au fond du jardin,
> Quand dans la nuit une invisible main
> Me terrassa plus forte que moi—
> Une voix me dit: C'est pour ta joie.

> I had gone to the heart of the garden,
> when in the night an invisible hand,
> stronger than me, struck me to earth—
> a voice said to me, It is for your joy.

Dilectus meus descendit in hortum . . . but here the poet, as chaste, is less sensual: The Orient has thrown a surplice over an Occidental soul, and if he still cultivates large white lilies in his enclosed garden, he has learned the pleasure of escaping, by secret paths known to fairies, "in the forest noiselessly laughing", as they gather bindweed, broom,

> Et les fleurettes aventurières le long des haies.

> And the tiny venturous flowers along the hedges.

This poem of twenty-four leaves is doubtless the most delicious little book of love verses given us since the *Fêtes Galantes*, and with the *Chansons d'amant* are perhaps the only verses of these last years where sentiment dare confess in utter frankness, with the perfect and touching grace of divine sincerity. If, in some of these pages, there still remains a touch of rhetoric, it is because Kahn, even at the feet of the Sulamite, has not renounced the pleasure of surprising by the ever novel deftness of the jongleur and virtuoso, and if he sometimes treats the French language tyrannically, it is that for him she has always had the affectionate yieldings of a slave. He abuses his power a little, giving some words meanings that hang on the skirts of others, making phrases yield to a too summary syntax, but these are mischievous habits not exclusively personal to him. His science of rhythm and mastery in wielding free verse, he borrows from no one.

Was Kahn the first? To whom do we owe free verse? To Rimbaud, whose *Illuminations* appeared in *Vogue* in 1886, to Laforgue, who at the same period, in the same precious little review—conducted by Kahn—published *Légende* and *Solo de lune*, and, finally, to Kahn himself; at that time he wrote:

> Void l'allégresse des âmes d'automne,
> La Ville s'évapore en illusions proches,
> Void se voiler de violet et d'orangé les porches
> De la nuit sans lune
> Princesse, qu'as tu fait de ta tiare orfévrée?

> Behold the rapture of autumnal souls,
> the town dissolves like near illusions;
> behold, veiled in violet and orange-hues, the portals
> of the moonless night
> Princess, what did'st thou with the jeweled tiara.

—and particularly to Walt Whitman, whose majestic license was then beginning to be appreciated.

How joyfully this tiny *Vogue*, which today sells at the price of miniature parchments, was read under the galleries of the Odéon by timid youths drunk with the odour of novelty which these pale little pages exhaled.

Kahn's last collection, *la Pluie et le Beau temps*, has not changed our opinion of his talent and originality: he remains equal to himself with his two tendencies, here less in harmony, towards sentiment and the picturesque, quite apparent if one compares with *Image*, that so mournful hymn,

> O Jésus couronné de ronces,
> Qui saigne en tous coeurs meurtris,

> O Jesus crowned with thorns,
> bleeding in every bruised heart.

the *Dialogue de Zélanae*,

> Bonjour mynher, bonjour myffrau,

> Hello mynher, hello myffrau.

as pretty and sweet as some old almanac print. Here, in the middle tone, is a truly faultless *lied*:

L'heure du nuage blanc s'est fondue sur la plaine
En reflets de sang, en flocons de laine,
O bruyères roses, ô ciel couleur de sang.

> The hour of white cloud is cast over the plain,
> like reflections of blood, like flocks of wool,
> O rose-coloured sweet-heather, O blood-coloured sky.

L'heure du nuage d'or a pâli sur la plaine,
Et tombent des voiles lents et longs de blanche laine
O bruyères mauves—ô ciel couleur de sang.

> The hour of gold cloud has paled over the plain,
> the long slow veils of white wool fall,
> O mauve-coloured sweet-heather—O blood-coloured sky.

L'heure du nuage d'or a crevé sur la plaine,
Les roseaux chantaient doux sous le vent de haine,
O bruyères rouges—ô ciel couleur de sang.

> The hour of gold cloud has burst o'er the plain,
> Gently the reeds sang under angered winds,
> O red sweet-heather—O blood-coloured sky.

L'heure du nuage d'or a passé sur la plaine
Ephémèrement: sa splendeur est lointaine,
O bruyère d'or—ô ciel couleur de sang.

> The hour of gold cloud has passed o'er the plain
> So swiftly: its splendour has vanished.
> O gold sweet-heather—O blood-coloured sky.

Words, words! Doubtless, but well selected and artistically blended. Kahn is before everything else an artist: sometimes he is more.

PAUL VERLAINE

Gaston Boissier, in crowning (touching custom) a fifty-year-old poet, congratulated him for never having innovated, for having expressed ordinary ideas in a facile style, for having scrupulously conformed to the traditional laws of French poetics.

Might not a history of our literature be written by neglecting the innovators? Ronsard would be replaced by Ponthus de Thyard, Corneille by his brother, Racine by Campistron, Lamartine by de Laprade, Victor Hugo by Ponsard, and Verlaine by Aicard; it would be more encouraging, more academic and perhaps more fashionable, for genius in France always seems slightly ridiculous.

Verlaine is a nature and as such undefinable. Like his life, the rhythms he loves are of broken or rolling lines; he ended by disjoining romantic verse, and having destroyed its form, having bored and ripped it so as to permit too many things to be introduced, all the effervescences that issued from his crazy skull, he unwittingly became one of the instigators of vers libre. Verlainian verse with its shoots, its incidences, its parentheses, naturally evolved into vers libre; in becoming "libre," it did no more than reflect a condition.

When the gift of expression forsakes him, and when at the same time the gift of tears is removed, he either becomes the blustering rough iambic writer of *Invectives*, or the humble awkward elegist of *Chansons pour Elle*. Poet by these very gifts, consecrated to talk felicitously only of love, all loves; and he whose lips press as in a dream upon the stars of the purifactory robe, he who wrote the *Amies* composed those Canticles of the month of Mary. And from the same heart, the same hand, the same genius—but who shall chant them, O hypocrites! if not those very white-veiled Friends.

To confess one's sins of action or dreams is not sinful; no public confession can bring disrepute to a man, for all men are equal and equally tempted; no one commits a crime his brother is not capable of. That is why the pious journals or the Academy vainly took upon themselves the shame of having abused Verlaine, still under the flowers; the kick of the sacristan and scoundrel broke on a pedestal already of granite, while in his marble beard, Verlaine was everlastingly smiling, with the look of a faun hearkening while the bells peal.

LITERARY CRITICISM

OXFORD LECTURES ON POETRY
Hegel's Theory of Tragedy, Wordsworth, Shelley. Keats, Shakespeare
A. C. Bradley

SHAKESPEAREAN TRAGEDY
Hamlet, Othello, King Lear, Macbeth
A. C. Bradley

FRIEDRICH NIETZSCHE
George Brandes

WILLIAM SHAKESPEARE - A CRITICAL STUDY
George Brandes

PROPHETS OF DISSENT:
Essays on Maeterlinck, Strindberg, Nietzsche, Tolstoy
Otto Heller

HENRIK IBSEN: PLAYS AND PROBLEMS
Otto Heller

EGOISTS: A BOOK OF SUPERMEN
Henry Beyle-Stendhal, Charles Baudelaire, Gustave Flaubert, Anatole France,
Joris-Karl Huysman, Maurice Barrès, Friedrich Nietzsche, William Blake,
Henrik Ibsen, Max Stirner, Ernest Hello
James Huneker

ICONOCLASTS: A BOOK OF DRAMATISTS
Ibsen, Strindberg, Becque, Hauptmann, Sudermann, Hervieu, Gorky,
Duse and D'Annunzio, Villiers de l'Isle Adam, Maeterlinck, Bernard Shaw
James Huneker

THE QUINTESSENCE OF IBSENISM
G. Bernard Shaw

THE SYMBOLIST MOVEMENT IN LITERATURE
Balzac, Gautier, Flaubert, Baudelaire, Zola, Mallarmé, Verlaine,
Huysmans, Rimbaud, Laforgue, Maeterlinck
Arthur Symons

& more

Check the website for more books
(new titles added weekly)

mannwilliam.org

Printed in Great Britain
by Amazon

22368841R00052